CHAOS to Clean
in
31 Easy BabySteps

By The FlyLady

Marla Cilley

Dedication

This book is dedicated to all the perfectionists who can't seem to get started. Jump in and please don't get stuck waiting for all the answers. Peace is just a series of BabySteps!

Acknowledgements

This book, as well as our website, emails, and social media presence would not be possible without everyone who helps me to support all of you! We are a team!

Buzz Words

5 Minute Room Rescue: A fun way to declutter your home

27 Fling Boogie: Another fun way to declutter your home

BO: Born Organized

Body Clutter: FlyLady's 2nd book and also the clutter in your mind and on your body

CHAOS: Can't Have Anyone Over Syndrome

Control Journal: A simple notebook that holds your routines

DD: Dear Daughter

DH: Dear Husband

DS: Dear Son

FLY: Finally Loving Yourself

God Breeze: A message from God

Hot Spots: A flat surface or chair that gets piled high with paper or clothes

Messages: This is the way we help retrain your mind. Join us at www.FlyLady.net

Missions: Every evening we send you a directive to do the next day

Mount Washmore: A large pile of laundry

Purple Puddles: This is when we cry happy tears

Reminders: On our FlyLady Messenger iPhone app, we send hourly reminders

SAHM: Stay At Home Mom

Swish and Swipe: A simple way to clean your bathroom in one minute

WAHM: Work At Home Mom

Weekly Home Blessing: Each week we bless our homes by doing seven things fast

Zones: This is how we break our homes down in doable sections

Are You Ready to Get Started?

I know that you have become overwhelmed by your home and the CHAOS (Can't Have Anyone Over Syndrome) that you have been living in. We are here to help you! Keep in mind that your home did not get this way overnight, and it is not going to get clean in a day. We are going to teach you how to take BabySteps and establish little routines for getting rid of your clutter and maintaining your home.

This system will work for anyone; it doesn't matter if you work outside of your home, stay home with children, are retired, or work at home. You can do this; you just need someone to pat you on the back and give you a great big hug to get you started. You have been living in clutter and CHAOS for many years; I do not want you to crash and burn. This is why I teach you to take BabySteps. If you try to do this all at once, you are going to be mad at me, because this will be like every other "get-organized" method you have tried. I want you to take your time. As you establish one habit, you will very easily be able to add another one to your routines.

So, what are the rules for BabySteps?

Establish small routines first and then work up to more items. Don't try to do a full-blown routine the very first day. FlyLady's routines are just an example to help you to develop your own. Pick three things for the morning and three things for the evening.

Consistency is the key to all of this. We have to take our time with our routines. They do not happen overnight. It is the result of tiny changes over several months. BabySteps! If you try to accomplish this without taking the BabySteps, your habits will not be everlasting. BabySteps are the key. Yes, you can do your routines by looking at a list of things to do, but they have to become automatic, a part of you, for them to be life changing.

Take your time and enjoy the process. Don't feel pressured to do it all at once. This is worth going slow. I did, and for once I didn't throw in the towel; I did it one habit at a time. When I did fall, I was able to pick myself up and start again at any time. It takes FlyBabies a month to establish a habit. Believe me, I have tried everything to not do this. Nothing ever worked for very long. It doesn't matter if you miss one day; just get back on your horse and keep taking those BabySteps. It is the practice that makes it work. Do not beat yourself up about this! Pace yourself!

Take your time with this! Don't go too fast or try to jump ahead. This is worth the extra effort to go slow. I know it is not in our nature to plod along. You are going to have to quiet this voice in your head and take it one habit at a time. Consistency has its rewards.

Are you ready to go from CHAOS to Clean in 31 Easy BabySteps?

DAY
1

Shine your sink!

Keep it clean and shiny.

Before bed, make sure it is empty.

Your First Assignment

You may not understand why I want you to empty your sink of those dirty dishes to clean and shine it, when there is so much more to do in your home. It is simple. I want you to have a sense of accomplishment. You have struggled for years with a cluttered home and you are beaten down. I want you to smile. When you get up the next morning, your sink will greet you and a smile will come across your lovely face. I can't be there to give you a big hug, but I know how good it feels to see yourself in your kitchen sink. This is my gift to you each morning. Even though I can't be there, I want you to know that I am very proud of you.

Go shine your sink!

Shiny Sink 101

Follow this procedure the first time you shine your sink. You do NOT need to follow this method every day. Just keep up the shine with a little window cleaner. I want you to smile from ear to ear when you gaze upon your shiny sink. I have heard every excuse in the world. Even old sinks can look new again with a little elbow grease. Here is how you do it: BE SURE AND RINSE WELL BETWEEN EACH STEP OF THE WAY!

1. Take all the dishes out of the sink.

2. Run some very hot water into the sink. Fill to the rim. Only do one side at a time. Then, pour a cup of household bleach into the hot water. Let it sit for 1 hour. Now, pull the plug with a pair of tongs. If you don't have tongs, then scoop some of the water out of the sink into the other sink and use your hand to pull the plug (wear gloves and don't get the bleach-water on your clothes).

3. Rinse your sink well.

4. Use some cleanser (Comet, Barkeepers Friend, Ajax, or Baking Soda) and scrub your sink. Be sure you rinse ALL of the cleanser from the sink.

5. Take a sharp edge and clean around the rim of the sink, just like you would clean dirt out from under your fingernails.

6. Clean around the faucets, too. You may need an old toothbrush or dental floss.

7. Now, get out your window cleaner, and give your sink a good shine. If it is still not shiny enough for you, then you could apply some car wax. This can help remove water spots and protect the sink. Just know in your heart that you have cleaned it very well. It doesn't have to be perfect. Our perfectionism is what got us in this situation in the first place.

8. Every time you run water in your sink, take your clean dish towel and dry it out (I lay out a clean one, every night with my before bedtime routine). Before you know it, you will be doing this every time you leave your kitchen. No more water spots. You will have a clean and shiny sink.

9. Don't have a fit if someone doesn't take as much pride in your sink as you do. It is very easy to fix. You have already done the hard part. You will never have to go through this process again. This simple daily habit will keep your sink shining, but nasty hurtful words cannot be wiped away. Be sure and tell your family what you are trying to do; they are not mind readers. They will think you have gone crazy.

10. If you don't have a dishwasher, don't worry. A dishwasher is just a dirty dish disposal unit. I have a solution: clean out a place under your sink and put a dishpan in there. Teach your family to put their dirty dishes in the dish pan, rather than the sink. Get into the habit of putting your dishes away as soon as they have been washed and are dry. No more leaving the dish drying rack on the counter or in the sink. Put it away under the sink when you have finished. If your old one is nasty, go buy a new set.

11. To make sure your family remembers this, put a note in the sink that will remind them where to put the dishes. Be patient! They have never been taught to do this, either. It is going to take some practice. "Thank you for putting your dirty dishes in the DIRTY DISH DISPOSAL UNIT!" You may want to add a smiley face to the note.

12. **One more warning: Please don't mix cleansers like Comet with Windex (or other ammonia based cleaners). You can create dangerous gases! It is worth repeating: rinse well between each step.**

A Blessed Moment of Insight

Dear FlyLady,

I've been a struggling follower for a long time, and when I read your stuff about perfectionism, I thought "Good heavens, how can I be a perfectionist? I've been messy all my life and forever sidetracked." Then, this week, a monstrous ah ha moment happened.

For a long time, I've kept my kitchen sink shiny, even when things get chaotic around it. Monday I came home from being away for the weekend, and found I had left a dirty coffee mug in the sink and one side had a coffee stain in it. I had an immediate sinking feeling that once again I had failed, that I may as well give up.

But from somewhere came a voice that said, "How absolutely, laughably absurd!! It will take less than a minute to fix that. You don't have to be perfect!" Since then I'm catching myself avoiding good routines because "It's a mess, anyway." You've talked about that awful "P-word" (perfect) over and over, but it took a blessed moment of insight to make it mean ME.

I'm not religious, but I'm quite willing to call that a God breeze.

Fledgling in MO.

"Shiny sinks in the morning help you start your day with a sense of peace!"

— FlyLady

Day 1

DAY
2

When you first get up:
get dressed to lace up shoes,
fix your hair, and face, too!

The Importance of Getting Dressed to Lace-Up Shoes

Many years ago I was a Mary Kay Cosmetic consultant. One main rule for the company was that you could not make a single phone call in the morning unless you were totally dressed, and I mean really dressed, all the way to shoes! The reason behind this rule was that you act differently when you have clothes and shoes on. You are more professional. The customer can tell when you don't feel good about the way you look. If getting dressed makes that big of an impression on someone who can't even see you, then what is going to happen to those who can see you; mainly yourself!

Putting shoes on your feet that lace up are better than slip-ons or sandals, because they are harder to take off. Instead of kicking your shoes off for a quick snooze on the couch, you actually have to go to a bit more trouble. Maybe in that short instant you will realize that there is something more that you can do. With shoes on those feet of yours, your mind says, "it's time to go to work." You have no excuse for not taking the trash out or putting that box of give-away stuff into the car. You are literally ready for anything that comes your way! Believe me, when you get that call from school that your child needs you, you are ready!

I don't want to hear that you say, "We don't wear shoes in your house." Well you do now! Go buy or clean up a pair just for that reason. It's not going to be you who tracks in the dirt anyway. You are still boss and you can require your children to remove their shoes. What is the problem here? In most homes you have had trouble even finding the floor, much less keeping the carpet clean. Teach your children to not track in stuff. Place a mat outside the door for them to remove unwanted dirt and mud. I'll bet you have ten pairs of shoes at the door right now. What does that do to your vacuuming schedule? Have the children take their shoes outside and clean them up, then put them in their bedrooms.

Butterfly God Breezes

Dear FlyLady,

I've been trying to fly for a while, and some things are working for me, but other things still haven't sunk in yet. I had an epiphany today and had to share it with you. This morning, when I was haphazardly going through my morning routine (I'm still having a hard time sticking to my list), I knew that I needed to pick out an outfit to wear. My closet is still cluttered, so it's not always the easiest task.

Something, maybe a God Breeze, maybe just the piled clutter in my closet, caused a pair of shoes to fall from the top shelf to the floor. They were a cute pair of black and white summer sandals with a decoration on toe. They had been hiding all winter on the top shelf. I remembered how much I liked the shoes, and decided to make my outfit based on the shoes. I found a skirt and top to match. (This was easier than usual because I've lost 20 pounds of Body Clutter so far).

I didn't give the shoes a second thought except to kick them off when I got home to relax (I know, I don't always wear my lace-ups) Of course, I began procrastinating, and not much has gotten done in the house this afternoon. That is, until I began reading my email.

I was reading the Butterfly emails one after the other, and was slowly getting motivated (I feel like the FlyBaby from Israel - I want out of my lonely cocoon, too!). I got up from the computer and started to pick up my room.

The first thing I picked up were the shoes I wore today - and I noticed that the decoration on the toes - while they look like flowers, are actually butterflies!!!!!

Someone is trying to tell me something! I want so badly out of this cocoon of clutter and body clutter - and I want to be able to let someone in my life. I know I can do this! And with your kind encouragement and reminders - and the encouragement from Above, I know I will succeed!

I am going to be that butterfly! Thanks so much for all you do, FlyLady and friends!

FlyBaby K in VA

"When my lace-up shoes are on my feet,

I feel empowered." — *FlyLady*

DAY
3

Keep your sink shiny
and continue to get dressed
when you get up each morning.

Keep Shining Your Sink for the Future

Today we are going to keep practicing shining our sink and getting dressed to the shoes.

Your shiny sink may just be the most important decision you ever make for your future! If a sink full of dirty dishes will cause you to spend money eating out when you have food in the house, then a shiny sink might actually help you release some debt.

Getting dressed to the lace-up shoes first thing in the morning is going to propel you into action. You are going to want to be productive. Putting your shoes on tells your brain that it is time to get down to business.

Shiny sinks in the morning help you start your day with a sense of peace! The sink is a tool in the center of your kitchen. When that tool is ready to be used at a moment's notice, we don't feel behind. We are not overwhelmed by having to do yesterday's dishes in order to put dinner on the table. My first habit was just to keep my sink clean and shiny.

When your kitchen is clean, then the rest of the house follows its lead. Before you know it, that little shiny sink habit has your house looking pretty good! And all you were required to do was keep your sink clean and shiny!

That shiny sink is going to give you patience, too. When your children want to help you make cookies, you will be excited about teaching them. This is such a blessing to you and to them. They will be learning skills that will prepare them for their future. You will be passing down your traditions. I learned to shine my sink from my grandmother. Are your ready to FLY?

Getting Dressed to Shoes Really Works

Dear FlyLady,

I want to share that I have always followed your get dressed to lace-up shoes rule. I think it is because when I was a child I grew up in mostly homes without carpet and so neither of my parents ever asked for us to take our shoes off.

Actually, I was quite poor as a child and grew up with an alcoholic step-father and 4 siblings so we had much bigger fish to fry than worrying about whether dirt got tracked in from outside!

Anyway, I wanted to share that because I follow your lace up shoes rule and so does the hubby - we have amazingly soft feet! It is so wonderful when you do finally kick off your shoes and socks at the end of the day and play footsies with your man or you and the kids rub footsies and everyone's feet are pleasingly soft because you protected them with shoes and socks!

Just a bonus from following wearing your lace up shoes - when I am able to treat myself to a pedicure the girl at the spa always comments how lovely my feet are.

Thanks FlyLady

FlyBaby on Cape Cod

> **"You cannot attack clutter**
> **unless you are**
> **dressed for the job."**
> *— FlyLady*

DAY
4

Place Post-It Notes

above your kitchen sink:

Get Dressed and Shine Your Sink!

We Don't Like Change

None of us like change. We are such control freaks and when we are not the ones implementing the change, we go bonkers. This is why gradual changes work so well for us. Our reminders help us to make these changes.

We are going to focus on building and using our own Control Journals. I didn't have reminders in my email when I started getting rid of the CHAOS in my life. All I had was my Post-it notes and checklists in my Control Journal.

We need reminders; this is why Post-it notes are so good. Place a couple of colorful reminders on your bathroom mirror to get you ready for bed and then to greet you in the morning. These will be the things you are practicing. When I was getting my home in order, I also had a checklist that would help me to remember all the things that I had to do each day. This checklist, in combination with the habits I was establishing, made amazing changes in my life and home. The BabyStep habits were my foundation.

A checklist is just that: a list of items that still need to be done. Even though we are not practicing specific items on that checklist, we sometimes just forget things. The idea was to not have to remember everything, but to glance at the checklist to see if we missed anything. Our minds were so busy that without the checklist, we might forget. Part of our habits is to remember to check our list and our calendar. You can do this, too. It is as simple as practicing a dance step.

Here is the part of my Morning Routine Checklist that is automatic:

1. Get up
2. Make my bed
3. Weigh
4. Shower
5. Get dressed to shoes
6. Fix my hair and face
7. Swish and swipe my bathroom
8. Put a load of laundry in the wash
9. Make coffee
10. Eat breakfast

All of these did not happen at once. Getting up and making my bed was paired together. Getting dressed and swishing and swiping was paired together. Laundry got me headed toward the kitchen to making coffee and eating breakfast.

These habits were not established immediately. I had to practice them. I like to call it piggybacking. When I got one habit established, I could easily sandwich another simple habit into the already learned dance step. I put them together into logical flow to start my day. One, two, three! One, two, three! One, two, three! Dancing on the FLY!

Basic Steps to my Daily Dance Routine:

1. Get up 2. Make bed 3. Go to the bathroom
1. Weigh 2. Check calendar 3. Shower
1. Get dressed 2. Fix hair and face 3. Swish and Swipe
1. Take vitamins 2. Turn on computer 3. Put on shoes
1. Check laundry 2. Fix coffee 3. Dust Mop the floors
1. Empty dishwasher 2. What's for dinner 3. Eat breakfast
1. Fill water bottles 2. Start my music 3. Sit down to work at the computer

Do you see how it all flows or shall I say FLYs by! One, Two, Three! This takes me about 20 minutes from start to finish because I have done my before bed routine and I am not trying to function in clutter.

My Control Journal became a place to hold my routines. I still had to be reminded when I was in the bathroom what the steps were. I am just like you! This is why I love Post-It Notes. I don't beat myself up because I need them. I have a morning one and a before bed one in my bathroom. This is where I start my day and end my day. I even keep my calendar in my bathroom. I use it to chart my weight and put appointments in red to remind me before I go to bed and when I first get up.

I Renamed My Routines

Dear FlyLady,

I'm a very new FlyBaby, but I had to write. I discovered your website when I bought a new planner a couple of weeks ago and began to watch YouTube videos on planner organization. A couple of the posters mentioned you, and I was instantly hooked!

I'm still working on building my routines, and taking BabySteps, but I'm starting to see progress. It's like losing the first few pounds at the start of a diet: seeing a difference in my house is so encouraging!

What I wanted to share (other than my gratitude) was how I write my reminder note in my new planner to do my morning and before bed routines. I don't call them that. I call them "First Flutter" and "Nightly Nesting"! It just makes me smile.

Thank you for making this seem manageable and reminding me that I CAN.

A grateful Flybaby in Tennessee

> ## "Our routines give us a different type of power! It is the power of peace"
> ### — FlyLady

Day 4

DAY
5

Recognize the negative things
you say, and now turn them
around to something good!

Are the Voices from the Past Paralyzing You?

I have found over the last few years that PERFECTIONISM is the main reason our homes are in this shape! PERFECTIONISM is the reason we are depressed and PERFECTIONISM keeps us from making things better.

We have been brainwashed our whole lives by our parents, teachers, and spouses that if you can't do it right, don't do it at all. So guess what? We didn't! I am trying to undo this stinking thinking and give you the freedom to just do something even if it is not the way your momma would do it.

What are the mindless words you hear in your head and whose face is saying these things? Next time you hear them, stop and ask yourself whose voice is that?

- If you can't do it right, don't do it at all. WHOSE VOICE?
- I can't possibly do this now; I don't have the time.
- I can't leave this unfinished.
- This house has to be cleaned all at the same time.
- That's not the way Momma did it.
- I can't shine my sink, because the dishwasher is already full.
- I can't lay out my clothes for tomorrow, because they are all dirty and I need to wash everything I own.
- I don't wear shoes in the house because my carpet will get dirty and we have babies on the floor. (Don't get me started with this one today, I am stopping myself, it is quite hard)
- Anything less than perfect is not acceptable. (this one has perfect in it)
- I can't start this system, until I have my control journal all set up.
- There are too many emails in my box; I don't have time to read them. (If I said this, I would never get anything done.) You think you have too many emails, you should see my inbox every day. I read one at a time and answer. All you have to do is read and delete at will.
- I haven't found the right planner yet.
- It takes me 3 hours to vacuum my first floor.
- I can't exercise during my morning routine; I will get sweaty and have to shower again. So exercise before you shower or don't do such strenuous workouts. Take a walk with the stroller or dance like no one is watching. Just do loving movements.

- I'm waiting until I get the perfect FlyLady shoes! Excuses! Excuses! Excuses! Wear what you have and get started.

- We are getting ready to move. I will start fresh in our new house. Not if your routines aren't in place. It will become the same pig sty you moved away from, you just took your bad habits with you.

- Oh and my favorite! It takes me too long to get dressed in the morning, that's why I stay in my sweats and barefoot. It takes you too long because you spend too much time thinking instead of doing. You are not going to the prom, just looking presentable to your family and yourself and whoever pops through your door.

My husband Robert had a wonderful Geometry teacher in high school. She taught him, "Anything worth doing is worth doing WRONG!" This is where I got my saying, "Housework done incorrectly, still blesses your family."

As Robert walked out the door one day, he said, "I just had a thought and it sent chills down my spine." I said, "WRITE!"

Do you hear your Mother's or Whoever's Voice saying, "That's not good enough, you can do better than that, go back and do it right!" It really didn't matter how nice a spin they put on it, the message came through loud and clear. "Anything less than perfect is unacceptable!" and the horrible extension: "Unless you are perfect, you are not good enough." or Not Worthy of Being Loved!!!

Is this what you have suffered with your whole life? Well I have news for those voices in your head. None of us are perfect! We have never been and we will never be. Quit striving for the unattainable. We are IMPERFECT BEINGS AND I AM THANKFUL FOR MY EVERY IMPERFECTION!

Now when are you going to Finally Love Yourself enough to say, "I cannot live with this any longer. I have got to stop."

Are you ready to FLY, Finally Loving Yourself? Let go of your Perfectionism and start to live without fear of being rejected.

What a Feeling of Relief

Dear FlyLady,

I have been flapping around for three years now and while I'm not flying swiftly, many of your routines have become habits and have helped me so much. Thanks for that.

I'm writing today with purple puddles rolling down my cheeks. I'm doing my master bedroom zone work of decluttering my dresser and closet. Now, I've done this before and I'm pretty good at it. The puddles today are because I'm really working at loving myself. The beautiful clothing that no longer fit me are finally going to bless someone else today.

I've struggled with my weight for a long time and my self-worth is very much attached to the number on the scale and the size on the tag. I've kept things for the someday when I'll be that small again. It occurred to me today that these things hurt me every time I look at them. So out they go. And with them, hopefully some of the negative thoughts I subject myself to daily. I know someone else will use these things and for that I feel blessed. No more skipping through things I can't wear anymore. What a feeling of relief. Thank you, FlyLady.

With love and gratitude,

A FlyBaby in NJ

"I want for you the peace that I have found!
You do not love yourself when you fill
your heart with negative feelings."
— *FlyLady*

Day 5

DAY
6

Let's find Hot Spots in the home.
It's any flat surface that
collects clutter. Clean it off!

Hot Spots Are Dumping Grounds

Is your home more than 15 minutes worth of messy? If you have lots of hot spots then I will answer this question for you, YES!

Our hot spots make our home feel and look cluttered. Why is it that we feel the need to fill up every flat surface in our homes? It is because there is an empty place to put something down. We walk in the door with our arms loaded and are desperate to unload; that is when we drop things in the first clear spot we find. It can be a chair, the counter top or even the floor.

Let's look at why we are trying to carry so much in the first place. We don't want to make a second trip to the car. Isn't that funny; we weigh ourselves down because we don't want to waste a few extra steps. I want to change your attitude about trying to carry too much and just make one trip.

We could all use a few more steps in our day. I have to walk up one level to get to our front door. Here is what I do when I get out of my car. I gather up all the trash and my purse or computer and head to the door. Then I go back to get anything else that is left in the car.

I do this with groceries, too. I take the refrigerated stuff first and put it all away and go back down for another load. Each time I come in the house, I put the groceries away. This keeps me from being overwhelmed. I don't like to see my countertops covered up with bags of groceries. Clear counters make me happy!

When our flat surfaces are covered up with stuff, we get overwhelmed too. If my coffee table is piled high with clutter, I can't write. A messy desk is not an example of a productive mind. It is a symptom of a cluttered mind. We have to stop and clear off the hot spot to get the clutter out of our minds so we can think.

Our poor babies deal with this problem, too. They have so much stuff in their bedrooms that they don't know what to play with. Get rid of the clutter and find peace and help them to enjoy their rooms. With less stuff, they will be able to better concentrate. With fewer things, we will be able to better focus on what we need to do.

FLYing Against the Wind

Dear FlyLady,

I've been a Flybaby for only a few months. In this time, I've made strong gains in establishing morning and evening routines, and have even gotten into the habit of getting my daughter to bed at a reasonable hour because I'm not scrambling around the house and stressed out about what I have to do tomorrow or the next day or later that week.

Then husband lost his job... I admit, I gave up and resorted back to old ways - the clutter accumulated, the hot spots raged - and I felt hopeless.

The other night, I was browsing through the archive of articles and I read several articles that all had the same message, "You are not behind! Don't try to catch up! Just jump back in!" Amazingly, this is the same message at the bottom of each of the daily emails! This gave me great encouragement. I cannot control when DH will find another job, but I can control my routines, the clutter, and extinguish those hotspots!

Yesterday I completed the daily mission, I de-cluttered for 15 minutes, I took 2 minutes each to extinguish a few hotspots, and shined my sink before bed. This morning I woke up to a tidier home and a better attitude to support DH in his new job search.

THANK YOU for helping me FLY again!

"Hot Spot Focus: Grab your timer, set it for two minutes and clear off the cluttered surface."

— FlyLady

DAY
7

Your Before Bed Routine.

Pick out your clothes for tomorrow

before you go to bed!

Your Before Bed Routine

Your Before Bed Routine is the most important routine of the day! It will start your tomorrow on a calm foot. Lay out your clothes for tomorrow.

In the morning, get up with the determination to get dressed as soon as your feet hit the floor. Get up 15 minutes before the flow of the family. NO EXCUSES! Fix your hair and face, so you can greet your day! Getting up and taking care of you is the most important job of your whole day.

Feeling pretty is more about your attitude. Sometimes our attitudes need a little help. I know many of you think that getting dressed is not important to keeping your home in order and getting rid of body clutter, but I want you to do this for me at first if you can't bring yourself to do it on your own. This system has never been about teaching you how to clean; it is about motivating you to get up and do just a little. I don't expect you to clean all day! Your simple routines will help you to maintain your home with just a few minutes each day.

My Granny always said, "Pretty is as pretty does!" As a child, I had interpreted this to mean that if you act right you will be considered to be pretty. Now that I am grown and I have finally started to love myself, I can see a whole new beautiful meaning to this unwritten law. If you don't treat yourself with respect and love, you will not feel pretty. Frumpy sweats have a way of telling our head that it is okay to eat that extra cookie, because no one will notice anyway. Before you know it, you will be filling out those baggy sweat pants. When you love yourself enough to only wear things that make you feel good about yourself, then you will not torture your body with clothes that are too tight and make you feel slouchy. Love yourself by just being nice to you. Try it sometime. You are worth it. Now don't complain that you are too heavy to feel pretty. Pretty has nothing to do with your weight! I feel pretty and I am not a size 10. Pretty is inside of each of you!

FlyLady's Before Bed Routine

The Before Bed Routine is the most important routine of the whole day. Set a regular time to do your Before Bed Routine, then do it, starting tonight. I start mine as soon as dinner is complete. Others start theirs in the afternoon while they are getting supper ready. It is up to you. There are three parts to my Before Bed Routine.

Clean up the house before you go to bed (Approx. 20 minutes)

1. Living room: pick up and put away things, magazines, dishes, clothes, shoes
2. Kitchen: clean it up, shine sink, lay out clean dishcloths, run the dishwasher
3. Dining room/entrance: clear the hot spots
4. Review checklist to be sure nothing has been forgotten

Think about tomorrow before you go to bed

1. Check your calendar and/or planner for appointments
2. Start a to-do list for tomorrow
3. Think: "What can I do tonight that will make tomorrow morning easier?"
4. Gather up items you don't want to forget and place them in a spot by the door that you'll see before you walk out
5. Make sure the children have their things put away
6. Start breakfast; set the table and plan what's for breakfast (mental note)
7. If you plan to use the slow cooker for dinner tomorrow, get some of the ingredients ready so they can just be thrown together in the morning
8. Lay out your clothes for tomorrow. It's a simple thing that saves time by being decisive. If something needs to be ironed or has a spot, you can deal with it calmly or choose something else. Take it to the cleaners, launder it, or fix that missing button according to your schedule – no pressure! All the stress has been relieved.

Focus on Yourself Before Going to Bed

Cool down time:

1. Get yourself ready for bed
2. Brush your teeth, wash your face, and comb your hair
3. Take vitamins and other meds
4. Bath time! Take a bubble bath or a warm shower
5. Put on your pajamas
6. Now you're ready for bed!

Reflect on today's accomplishments:

1. Listen to music. It doesn't matter what kind; just relax!
2. Pray or meditate
3. Snuggle in for the night and turn out the lights. Go to bed at a decent time, preferably the same time every night!
4. Fall asleep with a smile on your face and in your heart

Does that seem like a lot to you? Don't fret! Just start small. Do these three things, then build upon that to create your full-blown Before Bed Routine:

1. Shine your kitchen sink
2. Lay out clothes and put away other clothes
3. Brush teeth

Third Time is a Charm

Dear FlyLady,

I've lived in CHAOS my entire life, and am now thirty-two with a husband and two small children (age 4 and 6). About 5 years ago, in a conversation with my mother, she said that she wished she would have made me clean my room as a teenager, because it would have been better for my self-esteem, which has always been pretty horrible. That statement never made sense to me until I became a FlyBaby for the third time!

Third time is a charm, right? I've tried the FlyLady "system" twice before, but both times I let my perfectionism get in the way. My lists became long and intricately detailed, but they never got done. This time is different. I'm truly taking BabySteps, not letting myself get caught up in the marathon cleaning "binges" that used to start in the past when I would try to declutter for 15 minutes. I'm using a timer (yeah!), and with each day feel just a little bit better...not just about my home, but about myself. I am truly making the connection this time between how the state of my home is a reflection of how I am feeling about myself.

There is a bonus in all the home blessing that has been going on. This year, my six-year-old son was diagnosed with an Autism Spectrum Disorder. He is highly functioning, to the point that most people do not ever notice a difference between him and other kids his age. However, during his diagnostic interviews, it was stressed to me how important routines would be for him in determining his overall success in school, social situations, life in general. I immediately thought of your website and your emphasis on routines and came back for my third-round attempt. By maintaining routines for myself, it makes his routines even easier to establish and follow, and he is learning by my example. He is thriving. His "bad" days are becoming fewer and fewer, and he is finally learning independence and responsibility.

He has his own calendar, with the FlyLady student sticker set, that he checks every day. He knows, based on the stickers for the day, what to expect and what his routine for that day will entail. His self-esteem is increasing as well, as he learns that he is capable of doing the things he relied on me for. We are both learning to FLY. My four year-old old daughter seems to be born organized and has an amazing self-confidence level, but I know she is also learning from my example, and she too has her own calendar with stickers (because she was jealous that big brother got one) that she checks in the morning, and it is only a matter of time before my husband wants to be a part of this glorious FlyLady revolution happening in our home.

Thank you,

FlyBaby in Columbus, OH

> ## "Our routines give us a different type of power! It is the power of peace!"
> ### — FlyLady

DAY
8

Celebrate! I am so proud of you!

You have a simple

Before Bed & Morning Routine!

We All Love Presents

We all love receiving gifts: the thrill of the surprise of what is in the package; opening it up. Wouldn't you like to receive a special gift every single day? This is the gift that keeps on giving.

Your routines, even simple ones, can give you a great big present every day. There is nothing better than waking up to a home that surprises you each morning because it is CLEAN! I am still in shock when I walk out of my bedroom every morning.

This is the finest gift that I have ever received and the best part is I gave it to me! You know you deserve to have the thrill of this gift and it is so simple. But most of the time we are too busy beating ourselves up to take the few minutes to do our simple routines. We don't have time! We think every single minute of every solitary day is spoken for. In our perfectionism, we don't think we have time for anything new.

My question to you today is why did you buy this book if you are not willing to do the BabySteps?

So far all I have asked you to do is:

1. Get up each morning and get dressed to the shoes.
2. Do 3 BabySteps Before Bed Routine.
3. Go to bed at a decent hour.
4. Declutter your home for 15 minutes a day.
5. Shine your sink.

You really do have time: your perfectionism tells you that you don't have time! Let's look at how much time we are actually talking about:

Morning Routine

- Getting up and getting dressed to shoes 15-20 minutes

Before Bed Routine

- Lay out clothes for tomorrow   5 minutes
- Brush teeth   2 minutes
- Shine your sink   1 minute after it's done the 1st time
- Go to bed at a decent hour   0 minutes

Declutter Your Home   15 minutes

Less than 45 Minutes

Now 45 minutes at one pop may be too much to ask for but all I want is 15 minutes in the morning, 15 minutes to declutter, and 15 minutes at night before you go to bed. You can do anything for 15 minutes!

You are already getting dressed, just not when you first get up (unless you have to go to work, but I'll bet, even then, you wait until the last minute to get dressed). Getting dressed when you first get up starts you off on the right foot. Try it! You may be surprised by the difference it makes in your day. You may not be late to work any longer. This is the first gift you can give yourself: A stress-free start to your day.

Shining your sink may seem like a useless task that gains you nothing. If you feel this way, then you have not felt the pleasure of that sink greeting you in the morning. You see, it doesn't matter if your sink is stainless steel, porcelain, or thirty years old. It is not your reflection that makes you smile. It is the fact that there is not nasty water and dirty dishes shaming you each morning. I have been getting up to my shining sink since 1999, and I still smile each morning at my sink because it smiles at me first. This is a present I love to open every day.

Doing your Before Bed Routine of laying out your clothes and getting ready for bed may not seem necessary. After all, you are already going to bed. Why can't you just wait and pick them out in the morning? Because having them picked out and ready to go does not allow you to PROCRASTINATE about getting dressed. You have NO EXCUSE any more. A Before Bed Routine is the most important habit of the whole day. It is a gift that you wrap up in the evening, and you get to enjoy opening in the morning.

Are you still refusing to go to bed at a decent hour? Oh, you feel that this is the only time you have to yourself! Well, staying up late is robbing you of your health, patience and love. Not getting enough rest and trying to function on only a few short hours of sleep is not good for you, your marriage, or your children. Go to bed at a decent hour and give yourself the gift of FLYing!

I have had many people ask me what the most important part of the FlyLady program is. This is hard to say, but if I had to only pick one gift for you to give yourself, it would be to go to bed at a decent hour because you will be Finally Loving Yourself. If I can teach you that you need your rest, then your home will come together. You will no longer be dragging around living off of adrenaline. It all starts with you. I know you are looking for the magic solution to getting rid of the CHAOS in your home and life. The gift is there for you to open if you will only let go of your perfectionism and start with our simple BabySteps. No one is going to give you this gift but you. If you don't take care of you then who will?

Where Would I Be Without My Routines

There is something magical about the morning and evening routines. I feel such a sense of accomplishment throughout the day when I follow the routines. They are the grease that keeps everything manageable and flowing. I find that the routines are worthy of framing.

I bought three attractive, small, wallet-size, ornate, and embellished picture frames. I typed my routines for the morning and evening and printed those and put them in the frames. On one frame, I managed to fit both the morning and evening routines for my husband (his list is a little smaller). For our 8-year-old son, I used a larger frame that had the words "Focus on Little Things" etched in the glass and it hangs in his bathroom. I even have exercise included since it is part of my morning and part of husband's evening routine. A little heart represents cardio days and a dumbbell symbol reminds us when we do resistance/weight training. The morning frame is in the bathroom. My evening frame and my husband's frame are on the kitchen counter (among the very few items that are allowed to repose there). Although I have the routines memorized – I still need to glance at them a few times to keep on track. Having it in my brain is not good enough. Thanks for having us do routines – where would I be without them!

Flying Pretty in Texas, Miranda

> ## "FLYing is like opening up a present every single day! Are you ready to FLY?"
> *— FlyLady*

DAY
9

Let's Add Decluttering
to Your Morning Routine.
Try a 5 Minute Room Rescue
and 27 Fling Boogie.

Clutter on the Brain

The truth is getting rid of clutter is hard for everyone at first. It does get easier, but as with any new habit we are trying to establish, we have to practice. This is why I teach you to use some of our fun techniques to get rid of your clutter: 27 Fling Boogie or a 5 Minute Room Rescue.

In order to get the clutter out of your home, you have to first attack the clutter that is in your mind. Yes, our stinking thinking is what makes us believe that we will need this item someday and how could we even possibly live without having it in our home. The creative people that we are sees everything as a potential art project. There are just some things that are plain trash.

Then there is the "Ole Poor Me" mindset that does not give yourself credit for being able to provide for your family. This attitude is handed down through the generations because of the struggle our grandparents had during the Great Depression. There is also another side of holding on to things!

We are hoarding! By not releasing our unused items, we are being selfish with our excesses! Just how many can openers do you really need, not to mention linens, dishes, and furniture that is overcrowding your home? When we start to look at this type of hoarding, we see that we can bless others with our abundance. Then when we need something, it will be provided unto you. Your clutter is also filled with bad memories. Open up your door and toss those bad, sad, and depressive feelings out! I want you to smile when you walk through your home, not be reminded of sad times.

Sometimes we need games to get us into the habit of releasing our clutter. The 27 Fling Boogie was developed because I had lots of clutter to eliminate. The instructions for the 27 Fling Boogie are quite simple. Run through your home as fast as you can to gather up twenty-seven items to throw away. Then run through your home and gather up twenty-seven items to give away. Don't just stand there and hold them or stash them for a yard sale. When you have finished, put them in the trash or in your car to donate while you are running errands.

Day 9

The 5 Minute Room Rescue can be played two ways. I developed this because I had a room that was so cluttered that I was totally overwhelmed when I walked in there. I decided, if I was going to get this room livable, then I was going to have to make a rule. Whatever came out of that room could not go back into that room. I would push the door open just enough to grab a bag or box. Then I would take it into the living room and process what was in the bag. I had three piles: Give Away, Throw Away, and Put Away. I took the Give Away pile to the car. The Throw Away pile went into the trash can. Then I would put away the items that I wanted to keep. They had to have a place or I put them with the Give Away items. The other way to play the 5 Minute Room Rescue is to set your timer and just pick up and put away items that are out of place. Spend only 5 minutes per room. You will be so surprised at what you can accomplish in those few minutes.

Letting go of your clutter is difficult at first, but as you start to see a clear area, you will be empowered to do just a little more. Take BabySteps and you will find yourself practicing the art of flinging. It is so freeing to fling!

Making Up Games for Decluttering
Gets the Family Flinging

Dear FlyLady,

Today, I sent my girls to work on their closet for 5 minutes and they only picked up and put away 5 things in those 5 minutes. I realized the time periods of cleaning/decluttering didn't work for them. Instead we made a counting challenge. Our favorite game is the 100 item pick up. The three of us (my two girls and I) work together to pick up and put AWAY (very important, the items must return to their homes) 100 items. We use a dry erase board and markers to make tally marks every time we get 5 items put away.

You would not believe how much of a difference 100 items make (I just had to go search for 10 more items to put away, because the general mess of the day was already gone!) The most amazing thing to me is it usually takes us less than 10 minutes to do this! At the end of the day, or before we go to lessons and such, it helps so much. Just thought I would share an idea for anyone who has a hard time with the time period cleaning.

There are other ways to make it fun and get it done!

FlyBaby G in Wisconsin

> ## "If you make decluttering fun,
> ## it will get done!"
> ### — FlyLady

Day 9

DAY
10

Set a timer for 15 minutes and
gather all the trash in your home
and dispose of it.

The Power of 15 Minutes

We don't seem to grasp the simplicity of the timer. We automatically think (in our perfectionism) that keeping a nice house takes lots of time out of our day. We don't need a solid block of time (a whole day to clean) to have a home that is huggable. We just need 15 minutes.

All our lives we have lived in a frenzy. It is time that we stopped running around like a chicken with our head cut off and just focus. We are not racing the clock, trying to beat some world record. We just want to be consistent with our focus and take care of ourselves at the same time. Being in a frenzy is not healthy. We are looking for peace not panic.

The beauty of our timer is that we don't have to finish what we are doing. When the timer goes off, we get to celebrate what we have done and rest. Try it sometime! It is so calming. The timer is not a race! It is a focus.

The foundation for what we do is loving ourselves. This makes everything work. You are not loving yourself when you are running around in a frenzy! Slow and steady is what gets our home and our life in order. One BabyStep at a time. You can do this.

We don't think that 15 minutes will even make a dent in it. It will. You will be so surprised at what else will happen; it will give you confidence in your abilities. Some days I use my timer all day long. I worked 15 minutes on my book, and 15 minutes on a Morning Musing, and 15 minutes on the house. Then I spent 15 minutes taking care of me. Because, without those 15 minutes, I start to feel tired. I have to refresh my batteries each hour; drink some water, get up and move a little, put on some different music and go smell the flowers in the garden. This is taking care of me!

You put off gathering the trash because you think it is going to take too long to do it. Use your timer and gather your trash and take it out. It is a tool I could not live without! Take care of yourself and stop procrastinating by using your timer.

My Timer Stopped My Crash and Burn

Dear FlyLady,

I have been flying with you for over a year now. My home is peaceful and clean as a result of small consistent actions over 13 months. Thank you for your "Do It Now" principle and the 15 minute timer.

The way I've managed so well is by using your voice to remind me that I don't have to get it all done right now. Just 15 minutes here and 15 minutes there. And to look at myself and my home through eyes of growth NOT perfection.

This last year I have focused on routines (the first in my life!), decluttering, and loving myself and my progress. What worked best for me was to (1) break down your blessing hour into a small part for each day of the week. To (2) do laundry one load at a time between Friday afternoon and Sunday afternoon. And to (3) declutter. I broke the house into monthly categories to declutter. Wow! What a difference a year makes! And to (4) use short routines in the morning and at night. My bed is always made and my sink shined!

I have not as of yet had time to fit in the zone work but that is my next step. Since my house is so decluttered now I feel like that is the right thing to add in next. BabySteps, BabySteps, BabySteps!

I didn't try to do it all at once so I am still flying! No crashing burning for me because of your timer! Thank you for helping me do this 15 minutes at a time!

I feel proud of myself and proud of my home.

FlyBaby Erin

> ## "You can do anything
> ## for 15 minutes."
> ### *— FlyLady*

DAY
11

You can't organize clutter;
you have to get rid of it.

Clutter is Standing in Your Way

The reason we want you to declutter is that routines are so much harder to do with clutter standing in your way. Clutter has invaded all of your storage places. In order to put things away that are not clutter, you have to clear out your drawers, cabinets, and closets. My goal this year is to go through our home and declutter again 15 minutes at a time. Yes! You heard me right! Clutter has a way of sneaking back into your home. We have to stay on top of it. This is why it is so important to declutter 15 minutes each day.

Sometimes we have to be kind to ourselves during the process. We may not be ready to let go of certain things just yet. That is OK. One day you will be ready. Clutter comes off in layers; kind of like peeling an onion. The main thing to remember is don't do too much at one time. So set your timer for 15 minutes and start decluttering!

Things to ask yourself as you get rid of your clutter:

- Do I love this item?
- Have I used it in the past year?
- Is it really garbage?
- Do I have another one that is better?
- Should I really keep two?
- Does it have sentimental value that causes me to love it?
- Or does it give me guilt and make me sad when I see the item?

Get rid of the garbage! When the "Throw Away" box gets full, pull out the garbage bag, close it, and put it in the trash can.

When the "Give Away" box gets full, seal it off, and put it in your car. The next time you are out, you can donate to the area thrift shop. Do not save your clutter for a yard sale, garage sale, or eBay; you will be blessed by giving it away.

When the "Put Away" box gets full, take the box in your arms and run around the house (good thing you have shoes on – right?) and put the items in the room where they belong.

When the timer goes off, you have to put away all the boxes, but first you have to empty them all. Don't leave them in the middle of the living room floor! Go as fast as you can. You really can do this!

Decluttering is a Family Affair

I've just finished the BabySteps and have been decluttering excitedly. On the weekend, the whole family set the timer and did a 15 min declutter each. My friend, who told me about you, lets me know when she is going to declutter and we set our timers together and send a photo of the area before and after our 15 minutes. It's so much fun seeing what we've each managed to clear in that time.

Last night she was feeling tired and needed a motivational boost so I set the timer to see how much of my cross stitch project I could finish during her 15 minutes.

We also started using the Blessing Hour at our house on the weekend. The whole family got involved, though, so we're calling it the Saturday Blitz as it only takes us 15-20 mins to do everything! My kids are 9 & 12 so I write out a list and they just consult that and choose another job when they are finished the last one.

They've also started doing their own load of washing on the weekend so it saves me extra time for meal planning and prep!

Thank you for my newfound sanity!

FlyBaby Sherilee Melbourne, Australia

"You can't organize clutter;

you have to get rid of it!"

— *FlyLady*

DAY
12

Don't crash and burn
by allowing perfectionism
to take over!
Get our daily messages.

You Don't Have to Live this Way

Our procrastination is fueled by our perfectionism. We get caught in the trap of thinking we don't have time to do it right. This is when we do nothing. Eventually the procrastination bites us hard and our homes become overwhelming. Isn't this why you searched the Internet looking for an answer to your messy house?

We give you the tools you need. The most important part is the attitude adjustment. Just read what we write and use those messages to eliminate your perfectionism. It doesn't happen overnight. Your home did not become cluttered in a day and it is not ever going to be that "ideal" of "Perfect!"

Perfect is a myth you only see in pictures in magazines, social media, or Pinterest. It is a word that I despise because of what it does to my FlyBabies. We want to get it all together and feel good about our homes. We just never dreamed that in the process of getting our homes clean that we would find ourselves.

Our perfectionism, piggy-backed with procrastination, puts us in a coma. We don't know how to make a decision, so it is just easier to do nothing. Sometimes we just want someone to tell us where to start and what to do. I think this is why our message has touched so many people. We give you a starting place, then tell you that, you can do anything for 15 minutes.

In the time it takes to talk ourselves out of doing something, we could have the job done. You know the dialog. It has become invisible to our thinking processes because we have played it out over and over each time something needs to be done. We hear ourselves saying we don't have time. Those words are the first red flag for us. If you would set your timer for two minutes when you think you don't have time, "I don't have time" will turn into "Do It Now". This is 2 Minutes to Peace!

"Do it now" is doing something! Sometimes it is just putting away one item but it is something! Celebrate your "Go Me" accomplishments. They don't have to be perfect or even finished to be a reason to throw your arms up in the air and yell "Go ME"! Getting up is better than being paralyzed in a chair saying, "I don't have time".

It is time to stop procrastinating! You can do it! Just do something! You will feel better!

Inspiration Through the Eyes of a Three-Year-Old

Dear FlyLady,

While I am not sure that this is really a testimonial I wanted to write and tell you what happened at my house last night. I was depressed...really depressed. I am a struggling FlyBaby, although I am sure that I don't give myself enough credit. At any rate, I logged onto the website last night and as the screen came up I heard my Dear Son's (almost 3 years old) voice from over my shoulder.

"FlyLady! That's FlyLady!"

Looking at the picture on the website. (Now I don't have any of the other "fun stuff" from the FlyShop so the only way he knows about FlyLady is from the conversations he has heard me have with others. I think he once asked me who that was when I was on the website at another time.)

He continues with, "Oh, FlyLady! ... She's my friend."

Curious I asked, "Why is she your friend?"

"Because she loves me." he replied with a huge grin on his face.

"Yes," I said, "she does." I am tearing up just thinking about it. I realize that is why I keep trying. Even when I fall "off the wagon" or "crash and burn" I know that you will not judge me. I know you are there rooting for me, so I pick myself up and start again! I am a single mom and I have little to no support system. So, it may sound strange but I realized as I am writing this that I really depend on FlyLady. I know that you love me even though you don't even really know me; that you are pulling for me and probably even praying for me. Your love means so much to me!

Thank you! I can't tell you how often I have heard his voice in my head the past 12 hours. "Oh, FlyLady...she's my friend...Because she loves me!"

I am grinning just like he was with tears streaming.

Colorado Fledgling

> **"I'm going to love you
> till you get your wings to FLY
> all by yourself."**
> — *FlyLady*

DAY
13

Have you seen our daily missions?
You never have to spring clean again.

Dreading Spring Cleaning

As a child, we were forced to go through the torture of spring cleaning. We had to pull our furniture out of our rooms, wipe down the walls, clean out the kitchen cabinets and essentially turn the house inside out! When we would finish, we would stand back and look at the clean house. The sad part was, it was the last time we saw it clean, till we did this again; unless company was coming!

We have to let go of our perfectionism. When our homes were messy, we never got around to those things anyway. There is a chapter in my book, Sink Reflections: "You will never have to Spring Clean again!" We don't clean like our mother or even our grandmothers did. If you, will follow our zones and do the daily missions, you too, will never have to spring clean again.

For some people spring cleaning is a ritual for Passover. Many years ago, homes were heated with wood or coal. Soot got in every nook and cranny. This is why they had to marathon spring clean. Just because we don't clean our homes like they did doesn't make us bad housekeepers. After about three months of doing our daily missions, your home will be as clean as your grandmother's.

Here is the good part: we don't have to be mean to do this. All we have to do is spend a few minutes each day doing our missions. I have seen lots of yelling and screaming when children were forced into spring cleaning. Nothing was ever done to suit the mother. Do you want your children to remember cleaning this way? There is no wonder we have a dislike of house cleaning. Let go of your perfectionism and follow our zones; you will never have to spring clean again.

I Am Freed from the Clutter and CHAOS

Dear FlyLady,

I have been flying with you for 3 months now and my whole family is blessed with the change you have made in my life. (Myself, DH and 4 DS's. Having 4 boys under 9 was my favorite excuse...) I never liked housework before, put it off, made excuses and let chaos pile up. With your system and encouragement, I now really enjoy getting my house and myself slowly into order.

We recently came back from a week's holiday over Passover and boy was I happy to finally be back home and able to resume my routines! I desperately missed shining my own sink, keeping laundry under control, decluttering and moving forward in my quest for a home that I love to live in.

Knowing me only a couple of months ago, this is amazing. Passover was the easiest, most relaxed one I remember. The change is in my mind. Usually I would frantically try to declutter and clean the whole house in a couple of weeks. Feeling guilty when I didn't get the job done; I would leave everything untouched till next year. This year I knew I would keep on gradually decluttering as a routine. I wasn't under pressure because I can already see success

Just before Passover I took a whole car full of bags packed with unnecessary clothing to a charity. I couldn't believe I had so much "just in case" someone might want children's clothes or because it reminded me of when the kids were babies. The uplifting feeling of liberation as I drove home with an empty car is hard to describe. It was a true Passover experience - being freed from my own clutter and CHAOS that has had me enslaved for so long...

I am so glad I found you and thanks for blessing us,

FlyBaby in Jerusalem, Israel

> ## "It is so much fun to FLY
> ## without spring cleaning
> ## holding you down!"
> ## — FlyLady

DAY
14

Checking your calendar
keeps you organized.
Is your calendar big enough
for your family?

Stopping the Vicious Cycle

We all live such cluttered lives. We think that we do our best work under pressure. That is not and will never be true! This is just one of those lies we tell ourselves because we don't know how to stop the merry-go-round.

Have you been trying to juggle all those commitments in your head? We think we are so good at this! Why do we put ourselves through this day in and day out! We can learn how to handle our cluttered schedules by just looking at them on our calendar.

So, you don't use a wall calendar because you are good at keeping all this information in your phone. Or if you have one, you don't want to use it because you are afraid you will mess it up. This is our perfectionism reaching out to make the merry-go-round go even faster so we can't get off and take a break.

Seeing what is on our calendar is the first BabySteps to realizing that we have over-scheduled ourselves and our family. The second step is learning and practicing saying, "NO!"

I have a couple of tips when it comes to not being afraid of using your calendar:

1. Use colored pencils to write in your activities. Color-code each person.

2. Use small address labels to write activities; then put the sticker on your calendar.

3. Use the same address labels to cover up any mistakes or changes in your schedule.

4. Keep Post-It Notes handy to transfer information to your calendar.

5. Don't be afraid to make a mistake. More problems come from an activity not calendared than from one written down in a messy way!

Is your calendar large enough to hold all of your appointments? We sell a calendar every year that is big enough for everything: Menus, doctor's appointments, new school calendar, and best of all…your gold stars!

I promise, as each little habit becomes part of your routine, then you will begin to slow that chaotic ride down. It just takes a willingness to let go and grab for the golden ring of peace and quit whining that you don't have time!

Make It Fit Your Family

Dear FlyLady,

You wrote "The most important rule for using a calendar is to remember to look at it." I could never get my DH to do that until I found a place where he sees it first thing each morning, and the last thing before he goes to bed at night.

Uh huh, I hung it on the wall behind the toilet. It makes us both laugh, but it works. He remembers to write down his schedule every week and so do I. He hasn't forgotten a birthday or anniversary since it's been there either.

Thanks Marla and the FlyCrew, I love my calendar!

Flybaby Suz in CA

> **"The most important rule for using a calendar is to remember to look at it!"**
> *— FlyLady*

DAY
15

Add making your bed to
your morning routine.
Each room has a shiny sink.
Go make your bed.

Make the Bed Remodel

It is amazing how a made bed can change the whole look and feel of your bedroom. There can be hot spots on your night-stands and dressers burning away, but if the bed is made, the whole room feels and looks less cluttered. The bed in your bedroom is what the shiny sink is to your kitchen. If the sink is empty and shining, the whole kitchen feels better. The same applies to our beds. If the bed is made instead of the sheets and bedspread being in a tangled mess, it changes the way we feel when we are in the room. It is hard to make the bed when we don't feel good about how the bed looks. Maybe it is time for a Make Your Bed Re-Model! Take a good hard look at your bed and the bed linens to see what changes or improvements you can make.

Here are a few ideas:

- If you love the style and colors of your bedding, then strip the bed down and give everything a good washing. Pay attention to the care labels that tell you how to launder these items. Then remake your bed from the bottom up.

- Pillows – wash them or fluff them in your dryer. It is possible that your pillows will need to be replaced.

- Mattress – check your mattress pad if you have one – check to see if this needs to be replaced. Get someone to help you turn and flip your mattress if you have not done this recently.

- Do you have a different set of bed linens that you have not used in a while or that you have never used? Maybe change them out for a new look.

- Is it time to replace the current bed linens? There are so many new choices these days for re-doing your bed very inexpensively.

- Your bed is where you get the most important down time of all: sleep and relaxation for the next day. You deserve every night in your bed to be peaceful and comforting.

Look at your bed in the bedroom as importantly as you view the shiny sink in your kitchen!

My Husband Followed My Lead

Dear FlyLady,

With a couple of weeks of delay, I was able to master the habit: making the bed every day. If truth be told; it was nice to enter the bedroom in the evening and be welcomed by a calm and relaxed atmosphere. It does require some discipline though. I get up about an hour before my dear husband and it requires me to consciously go back into the room before leaving the house to make the bed, but I'm loving it!

Do you know what happened this morning? I went back up to our room and found the bed all made up by my husband! I texted him with just a couple of xoxo. My guess is he doesn't even realize why I did that.

Thanks, FlyLady, I have to admit I've been skeptical that all this blessing my house would be returned to me by family members, but hey. It's seems to have started, BabySteps.

FlyBaby C in Belgium

> ## "Your bed is your
> ## shiny sink of the bedroom.
> ## Make it every day."
> ### — *FlyLady*

DAY
16

Read a Morning Musing.
Our messages simply
change your thinking!

Stopping the Noise in our Minds

We all deserve to spend a little time to ourselves. When was the last time you did that? I am not talking about taking a vacation alone; I just want you to sit quietly with your thoughts. Oh, that is a scary thing for you! I know how hard it can be. Why do you think we turn on every machine we have in the house? That includes television, radio, computer, and phone. We need noise so we don't feel alone.

My Sweet Darling calls it yammer. Do you want to know what yammer does for us? It keeps us from having to listen to those negative thoughts we have in our head. No wonder we don't want to have quiet around us. The yammer is camouflage for our brain.

Yammer also keeps us from listening to our positive inner voice; I like to call this God Breezes. It was only after I quieted the negative voices, turned off the yammer, got rid of the physical clutter and found myself in a quiet space that I was able to hear and respond to the God Breezes that were sent my direction.

Until that time, I was so busy putting out fires that I didn't have a spare moment to think or even reflect on what was going on in my life. I was in a reaction mode and not in act mode.

I want you to practice one little thing for me. Take 5 minutes and clear off a hot spot, then turn off the noise in your home. After that, I want you to sit with a pad of paper and a pen, then quietly take notes on what you hear in your mind. Set your timer for only two minutes. This can be interesting.

Releasing the Negative Voice in My Head

Dear FlyLady,

Thank you for the years of encouragement. I am at the beach for a week for a much-needed break from caring for my elderly mother and a disabled sister. It has been two years since I was last here. I am at a little old fashioned beach house right on the beach (high tide brings the ocean almost to the deck). The porch is complete with picnic table and three old army cots. I have "staged" the house-complete with white old fashioned linens on the tables and white spreads on the beds. The table has a white tablecloth and fresh flowers. It feels so good to take care of myself and not feel guilty about it. Thank you for that.

A little while ago I decided to ride my bicycle down the beach. I haven't been on it in two years since I was last here. Even on the flat terrain, my thighs were screaming at me to stop. And then it hit me-use the 27 Fling Boogie Principle.

So, I counted each time I took a downward pump with my right leg-after 27 strokes, I coasted. WHAT A HOOT!! I feel like a kid. I had to stop back by the house and write to you. I was just zooming down the beach and having a blast. Before FlyLady, I would have done the negative self-talk about how out of shape I am (even though I have recently lost 40 pounds) and would probably have ridden about a block, turned around and parked the bike for the rest of the week, gotten into the car, and driven to the store to stock up on junk food so that I could forget about what a wretched human being I am. But not now-the positive words from you over the years have Fly-washed me and I was able to stop the negative voices and turn the bike riding into a game and have a good time.

Thank you so very much. I am going to grab some water and go back out for a bike ride.

A 55-year-old beach baby, FlyBaby

> **"We teach you how to become**
> **your own cheerleader and to**
> **ignore the nay-sayers in your life!"**
> **— *FlyLady***

DAY
17

Establish a bedtime!

Put it on your Before Bed Routine!

You need 8 hours each night!

Are You Sick and Tired of Being Sick and Tired?

Your bedtime routine is the most important in my opinion, because it gives your morning a head start. Your dishes are done, the house is picked up, and hot spots are under control if you do a very simple Before Bed Routine. But this can all be thrown right out the window if you stay up till the wee hours of the morning.

Those of you that are doing this are hurting yourself and your family. I can hear you now, "this is my only time to myself!" Well to this, I say," A little is good, a lot can hurt!" You have to get the rest that your body needs or you are not going to feel like doing anything the next day. This is one of the reasons that I think our homes got in the shape they are in: Not enough restorative powers of a good night's rest.

Sleep lets your mind take a break, your cells rebuild, and your eyes rest. Without enough sleep, you wake up unrested, feeling sluggish and in a bad mood. You know about those bad moods. They rear their ugly heads, and words come out of your mouth that you wish you could take back. Hurtful, non-patient words that effect your children, husband and your lives. Many of our members have health problems, and sleep is so important to the healing of our bodies. Lack of sleep can even cause us to get sick.

I believe with all my heart that getting the proper amount of rest is essential to having a home run smoothly. I don't want to hear that I only need 4 hours sleep and I am fine. THIS is not true. You may be able to function, but at whose expense? Your family's, not to mention yourself?

This has got to stop. I have tried to remind you to go to bed at a decent hour, but you all get wrapped up in many things and don't want to listen. Have you ever read a book till you could not hold your eyes open? I have done this. It is our obsessive behavior that will not let us put the book down. Another obsessive thing we do is binge watch shows on television. But the main reason is social media; I am afraid that we are letting this get in the way of our happy organized home. If you have babies, you are going to miss some sleep, but do what you can to rest when they rest. Your body will thank you later.

As I said before, a little is good, a lot can hurt. When we stay on social media all day and all night, something has to suffer. The brightness from the display plays with your brain's day and night signals. This is why I never look at my phone, television, or my computer in the middle of the night.

That device you are looking at right now is a tool, only a tool. It is there for your convenience. When you allow it to interrupt your day and your nights, you and your family are the losers. Communication is the first thing to leave. You are no longer talking to your husband or your children. You are wrapped up in everyone else's lives. I know that you are using the device to get your home organized, but you don't have to be on it all day. I am preaching to myself right now as much as to you.

In a perfect world, we would get our morning routine done and then check social media for a few minutes as a reward. Then put it down so we could do other things. At lunch, we could check in again and put it down after lunch. Dinnertime is family time. Your focus is on them. Place a basket on your table for all of your phones. We have to get a handle on this problem.

Think about what we are doing to ourselves, our family, and homes. Make a commitment to me and to yourself to get more sleep, listen to your body cry out for rest and cut down on social media time. You will notice the change almost immediately.

A Wake-Up Call

I have subscribed to your messages for a long time, and while there are still many aspects of your program that I have yet to incorporate, my life has improved immeasurably because of the changes you have inspired. One thing that I have not been able to do consistently is get to bed at a decent hour every night. As of today, however, that has changed.

Since I often stay up until the wee hours I am frequently sleepy during the day, especially while driving. I have known for a long time that someday it would get me into trouble. This morning while driving with my 6-year old son in the car I dozed off long enough to run off the road ON THE OTHER SIDE FROM WHERE I WAS DRIVING. I woke up just in time to avoid hitting a wooden fence and was able to steer back onto the road without further incident. I pulled over and checked the car for damage, and when I got back into the car my son said "Let's not do that again!"

I cannot emphasize enough how lucky I am. Although I was driving 55 mph, I was on a very uncrowded rural road. I'll probably need a front-end alignment, but other than that my car is undamaged. Most importantly, my son was unhurt and not frightened (because he didn't really know what happened). I was also not hurt, and I consider the fact that I was terribly shaken by the event to be a tremendous gift. Beginning tonight, I will be going to bed at a decent hour no matter what remains to be done or how much I feel like I need some time "to myself". I may even get a little car-shaped charm to wear so that every time I am tempted to stay up too late I can be reminded of my near-miss. I don't EVER want to forget how awful this was or how fortunate I am.

Thank you for everything you do for all of your babies out here, and for giving me the tools and the mindset to turn my bad experience into something that will actually benefit me and my family greatly.

Love,

A VERY Lucky Central New York FlyBaby

"Taking time for yourself
not only blesses you
but also blesses your family."
— *FlyLady*

DAY
18

Check out my 11 Commandments!

Simple rules to live by

Finally Loving Yourself!

List Maker, List Maker

We all love lists. We make them every day and look at them. Lists can be helpful or they can make us feel bad. It is up to us to use the list to empower ourselves. We have top 10 lists, tips on every magazine cover, and let's not forget about the 10 Commandments. I have even made my own list of FlyLady's 11 Commandments.

This little list gives you the tools to find peace in your world. Just reading the list is not going to give you the answers to all those questions. But guess what? It is a great start. I know why we love lists so much. It is because they seem so easy and we have time to read a list. So here goes. I am going to take our 11 Commandments and show you how doing them is a way to pamper yourself every single day. It is the being nice to yourself that is the key to this peace!

1. **Keep your sink clean and shiny!** This puts a smile on your face and helps you to stay on top of our kitchen.

2. **Do your Before Bedtime Routine EVERY NIGHT.** Doing a before bedtime routine helps you to start each morning on a good note, not running through the house in a screaming fit. Everyone deserves to wake up without stress.

3. **Do your Morning Routine EVERY DAY, RIGHT WHEN YOU GET UP.** I Want you to dress to lace up shoes so that you look good and this will help you feel well, too.

4. **Don't allow yourself to be sidetracked by social media.** We have a tendency to stick our heads in the sand. Let social media time be a way to pamper and reward yourself.

5. **Pick up after yourself. IF YOU GET IT OUT, PUT IT AWAY WHEN FINISHED.** This is one thing that we don't even notice until it goes undone. When picking up after yourself all the time becomes a habit, you no longer have major hot spots to make you feel bad.

6. **Don't try to do two projects at once. ONE JOB AT A TIME. Don't pull out more than you can put back in 1 hour.** Getting overwhelmed by a project is not good for your stress levels. Focus on one thing and you will find peace.

7. **Do something for yourself every day, maybe even every morning and night.** You are worth it!

8. **Work as fast as you can to get a job done.** This will give you more time to play later. Free time is me time! Don't let a job hang over your head. Get it done and forget about it.

9. **Smile even when you don't feel like it. It is contagious.** A smile on your face can change your whole attitude. Do it even if you don't feel like smiling. The smile tells your head that you are happy. You can do this.

10. **Make your mind up to be happy and you will be.** We can talk ourselves into anything: Why not happy? Get out of your ole poor me attitude and count your blessings.

11. **Pamper yourself, you deserve it.** Yes, you do. You do so much for everyone else, take a few minutes to do something nice just for you! When you develop the habit, you will be FLYing High!

I want pampering yourself to become just as automatic as putting on your shoes and shining your sink. If you don't take care of you, then who will! I want pampering to become a way of life; every single day! I think you just need to be given permission to do this. Maybe not even permission, but an order! Now go pamper yourself.

Taking the Time to Have a Relaxing Meal

Dear FlyLady,

I just wanted to let you know how rewarding your 11 commandments can be. "Do something nice for yourself" is the one I obeyed today and it was so enjoyable. I'm going to do it more often!

We live in a very small city and I often go to a larger city to shop (1 hour away). I was making such good progress with my FlyLady Control Journal that my 2-year-old daughter and I had lunch at a real restaurant with real silverware and cloth napkins. It only cost $13 counting the tip (soup and salad).

It was nice to take a moment to just sit down and relax. My inner child even enjoyed coloring with my child at the restaurant. I always thought I didn't have enough time to sit down for a real meal. I was too busy buying too many clothes or too many scrapbooking supplies. Not only was it enjoyable but it was so much healthier than the fast food we normally scarf while driving to our next stop. I didn't have that smelly fast food garbage in my car to deal with later and no crumbs, and no spilled drinks.

I even beat my husband home from work and had all the groceries put away with time to spare. My biggest delight was finding my home orderly (not perfect just orderly) thanks to some pre-planning like the launch pad and the morning routine.

I'm so excited about the flying. I have great plans to soar like an Eagle. Thanks for all you do to inspire me!

Fluttering FlyBaby Marie in Alabama

"If you don't take care

of you, then who will."

— FlyLady

Day 18

DAY
19

Are you ready for your home

to feel like a vacation get-away?

Looking for Your Vacation Get-Away

What is it about going on vacation that makes it worth all the preparation and hassle? Is it getting away from the phone? I don't think so; most of us have our personal cell phones. Is it getting to seeing new places? Maybe but many of us usually want to go back to old familiar areas. Is it the food or that cooking in an efficient clean kitchen is easy. How about the people? They are the same ones you have at home.

So what is it about being in a different place with the same people? Could it be that the surroundings do not choke you! Hotel rooms are sparse: Two beds, a desk, one bathroom, a night table, one small closet, a little dining table and maybe a little refrigerator. Hey, I am leaving the television and video games out. Ignore them.

Let's say you rent a condo at the beach. It has a small kitchen, two to three bedrooms, a living area, a balcony, a couple of bathrooms and empty closets. The same thing for a house at the lake or a cabin in the woods; they have all the conveniences of home without ALL YOUR CLUTTER!!!

Oh it's not clutter it is your stuff, you may be yelling at me. Well your stuff makes you feel like you need to leave home to breathe. What does that tell you? Your stuff is killing you. You are uneasy in your own home. Another word for uneasy is disease. Get it? Your house has become a storage unit for your stuff, not a home. This is why it feels so good to walk into a sparsely decorated room. The space frees you to breathe without you feeling closed in.

This is what it is going to take to get your home feeling like a vacation get-away. It is called a feeling of peace. It doesn't happen overnight, but you can begin to get that calm feeling by taking a few BabySteps to get you on the pathway to peace. You can do this. We have seen millions take this first BabySteps. Peace is a journey not a destination.

My 5-Star Epiphany

Dear FlyLady,

My first testimonial and opportunity to add my thanks for all that you do in helping all of us FlyBabies.

My husband and I decided to have a "Date Night" at a 5-star hotel last weekend and, while we had a lovely time, we kept comparing it to our "resort" that we live in 24/7. Thanks to you we have everything a 5-star hotel offers and more, all at our fingertips. Thanks to you I have slowly replaced my ratty towels with nice ones, have planned scrumptious breakfasts that are still healthy, and serve them on our deck that is clean and inviting so we can look at the birds and enjoy our garden.

Your "do it now" principle means that we don't have to have crisis cleans of the house or yard as it all looks pretty good most of the time. It also means that we keep our house maintenance up to date and everything works like it should.

Last week we were happy to offer our guest room to a friend and, after visiting the hotel, decided we offered at least 5-star accommodation-a clean, sweet smelling bathroom, lovely clean sheets and pillows, and I put out a couple of little "extras"-a new toothbrush, toothpaste and a new disposable razor in a clean cup as well as the shampoo and soap in the shower. The pantry was well stocked, our meals were planned so we could cook easily and still have time to visit, and the living room was inviting for relaxing, with or without the television.

So while a night out at a hotel was fun, since our kids are grown having a Date Night at home has become even more attractive since we know that we have everything a hotel offers and more space than the standard hotel room. And we can splurge on a bottle of wine, DVD, or special meal ingredients and still save money.

Thanks for teaching me to declutter and to set up my own 5-star "resort" so I can treat my husband and myself to the "special guest" treatment at home.

Barbara, Brisbane, Australia

"FLYing is a process of establishing habits that will transform your home from CHAOS to the tranquility that changes your life" — *FlyLady*

DAY
20

Laundry stands
in the way of FLYing!
Doing a load a day keeps
Mount Washmore away!

Laundry, We All Have It

Do you feel like you never get finished with the laundry? Is there evidence of the laundry process all over your home? Are there soured towels in the washing machine because you forgot about them? Do you have a dryer full of wrinkled clothes because you were on the phone when the buzzer went off? If you actually folded them are they still on top of your dryer or piled in your laundry basket waiting to be put away?

Laundry is just like dishes. If you eat on plates and drink water out of glasses, you will have dirty dishes. If you get up and get dressed and get ready for bed, you will have dirty clothes. Dishes or clothes don't magically get clean; someone has to lift a hand to start the process. Starting the process is just the beginning of a five-step journey to climbing Mount Washmore!

One day you wake up to no clean underwear. So, you either have to go buy some new undies or do the laundry. By this time, you have worn every clean item of clothing you have and Mount Washmore seems like Mount Everest. Where do you start?

If your laundry has gotten out of hand, there is a good chance that you do not have a routine for staying on top of it! I am going to teach you how to get it done and then give you a routine for keeping up with it.

We are going on a laundry scavenger hunt. Put on some fun music! Go to your laundry room and check the washer and dryer for forgotten clothes. Start sorting those clothes into piles: whites, delicates, colors, jeans, towels, and sheets. Then check your laundry hot spots: the bathroom floor and hamper, treadmill handlebars and the bedroom chair. You know your favorite dumping ground for dirty clothes. Get the children involved, too. Ask them to look under their beds and in their closets. Keep sorting the clothing into your piles.

Next, gather up all your laundry baskets and put your laundry detergent, softener and stain pre-treater in one basket. Then go to all your closets and gather up all the empty hangers and put them in another basket. You have lots of piles of clothes. Put single loads in garbage bags and take them to your car. You probably have ten or more loads. The next thing you are hunting for in this scavenger hunt is money. Go cushion diving or to your change jar to gather up coins for the laundromat. Now don't fuss that you have a washing machine and a dryer. You have not been using them. It is time to get this done!

Before you leave the house, clean out one drawer for each family member. Most of the clothes in your drawers you do not wear because if you did they would be in the dirty clothes bags. So, put them in a give-away bag. This way, when you get home from the laundromat, you will have a place to put your clean clothes. As you are folding the clothes at the laundromat, don't fold things that you don't love or that does not fit. If it is too stained to give away, then put it in the trash. Have a give-away bag handy as you are doing your folding. Don't take anything home that is just going to become a stumbling block to your daily routine of doing the laundry.

A load a day keeps you from having to scale Mount Washmore! Don't wait till you are overwhelmed.

I Climbed Mount Washmore and Survived

Dear FlyLady,

I want to start with a thank you. I started following you about four months ago. I have a long way to go, but I can see so many changes not just in my house but in me. I am trying to get my friend to Fly as well, but it does have to come from inside you.

I just want to give you one example of how my life has changed in a very "monumental" way! Every day I say to myself..."A load a day keeps Mount Washmore away"! Four months ago, I had laundry piled so high in my laundry room it was hard to walk through to get to the garage where we exit. That "pile" extended into my hallway and down it. More often than not, if I walked to my boys' room I was pushing laundry aside. I had a huge pile of clean laundry waiting to be folded on my dining room table and that often spilled over onto my couch and chairs in the living room. That was my life for a long time.

Then this last September I decided to work on just one load a day. Yes, I did a few more on some days. To get the laundry folded I started setting my timer for 15 minutes at a time. None of this killed me or even felt slightly bad. My hallway cleared out. I started to see my dining room table again. But I was still battling; not as much the dirty piles but the clean piles. I got my clean laundry down to two baskets in my bedroom that were always piled high, but that was starting to change too.

What I had to do was get my closet decluttered as well as my boys' closet, and anywhere else laundry belonged. I did all of that 15 minutes at a time. I still have some areas and they keep getting better. I folded my socks, and my drawer has enough room to put those sock in. My closet has a place for everything. My kitchen towel drawer holds just kitchen towels and no longer other junk. I have finally cleaned off the tops of my washer and dryer and my laundry baskets go on them.

Today, I no longer live under the weight of Mount Washmore. It was a hike! It took me four months to conquer it. The best thing about it, I no longer dread doing laundry. Most loads can be folded and put away in 5-10 minutes. There is a place for everything and I make it a point to keep tossing out what I no longer use or my family no longer uses. I am no longer a slave to laundry but it is an enjoyable part of my life. Even if there is an "accident" in the house; an extra load no longer feels like climbing to the top of a mountain in just one day or wading through that mountain to get down the hall or to my car!

This is just one area of my life. No more crashing and burning for me! Thank you! Onto my next 15 minutes!

FlyBaby Nancy

"Nothing says I Love You

like clean underwear."

— FlyLady

DAY
21

Every day I answer a question.

We are here for you!

Your Questions are My Inspiration

Over the years, I have answered every type of question you could think of. Questions and answers are one of my favorite parts of any speaking engagement. Did you know that I answer a question every day on our website and it goes out in our daily messages?

Do you have a question? I would love to answer it. You can email me at FlyLady@FlyLady.net, ask a question on our Facebook page, or ask a question when I do a live Facebook video. We also have several years of podcasts archived on our website for your listening pleasure. When we did our podcasts for several years, I answered two hours of questions. Your questions are fuel for me! Please don't hold them back. Every question always helps someone else. I am here for you!

A Blessed Moment of Insight

Dear FlyLady,

I am listening to your radio show archive right now, and I am hearing you say to a caller that if she gives the children's old clothes away she will be blessed when they start to need clothing.

That is so true! One year ago, I was paralyzed about giving away old clothes. You answered my question on "Ask Flylady," and you encouraged me in the same way.

Every time I come across an article of clothing that is stained or torn, I throw it out. Every time I see something too small, I toss it from the laundry straight into a basket I leave by my dryer. And most every month I have a bag or more to donate to my church's clothing drive. Every three weeks, I go through one of my kids' drawers and make sure that child has 6 everyday and 2 dressy outfits, 8 socks, 8 underpants, and a jacket or coat that fits. I am so proud of me!

And here is the best part. I seem to have an abundance of clothes! When people offer me hand-me-downs I say, "Thanks, but only if you'll let me bless others with what we don't need right now." Everyone is happy to agree to that condition and when I think a child needs something, I write down the need and I force myself to wait a week or two. I find that I am buying so little.

I can't thank you enough for teaching me to step out in faith and FLY!

New Jersey FlyBaby with 3 well--outfitted little ones under her wings!

"The only stupid questions

are the ones that

remain un-asked!"

— *FlyLady*

DAY
22

Has perfectionism
stopped you from making
a Control Journal?

Rome Was Not Built in a Day

Our impatience sets us up for failure! This is because of our crash and burn syndrome. We push ourselves too hard in the beginning; you know how this works. Our perfectionism expects us to get a handle on our homes in no time at all!

This is why I keep telling you that your home did not get dirty in day and it is not going to get clean overnight. Anyone who thinks this is going to happen needs to sit down and have a reality check. We have been living in chaos most of our lives.

At first the chaos was just in one small area of our home and slowly it took over every part of our lives. Chaos breeds more chaos. But here is the miraculous component of our FlyLady routines: as you establish one habit, that habit causes chaos to retreat just a little.

As chaos recoils to your hidden areas, you begin to feel a little ray of hope. That hope gives you courage, your courage gives you energy, and before you know it your wings are sprouting! Everything you touch makes you smile and that smile is what it is all about!

This doesn't happen in a few hours; we have to establish simple little habits to help us. FLYing is more contagious than chaos. Chaos tries to sneak up on us every chance it gets. We are aware of it now and can get out our FlySwatters to keep it at bay!

The best FlySwatter we have is our Control Journal. This is just a simple instruction manual for your home; a binder to hold your simple routines. A caterpillar doesn't become a butterfly overnight. Rome was not built in a day and your homes are not going to be magazine picture perfect just because you found this FlyLady person. We have to exercise patience with ourselves. Patience is kindness! Please be kind to yourself and you will be sprouting your wings. Are you ready to FLY with your favorite FlySwatter in your hand to keep CHAOS away from you?

Your System Works Wonders

Dear FlyLady,

There I was, starting to really Rock my Routines, and it felt fantastic! My house was almost completely decluttered, and it was clean! I was even mastering the hot spots, which I always thought I was too tired to do before bed. While I was procrastinating in my mind about it one evening, I realized I was cleaning off a hotspot while whining that I didn't have the energy to do it. With my routines in place, I didn't realize I was actually doing it automatically! I was SO happy!

That's when it all came crashing down and burning at my feet. My mind said, "This is so easy, I can do MORE! With FlyLady's system, I'm only deep cleaning one zone a week, which means it only gets done once every five weeks. THAT'S NOT GOOD ENOUGH! I know. I'll do one zone every day. I can spend just one hour a day on each zone and the house will be PERFECT all the time!!!"

You know the rest. The routines fell away after I would miss a day here and there, then fell behind on everything and now I'm completely out of my easy routines. I have to start all over building my routines and opening my control journal again.

Your routines, when they truly become routines and we don't think about them, made me think it was so easy. My perfectionism made me think I could and should do more.

Your system works wonders. We don't feel like we are doing anything and the house is sparkling. Next time I get into my routines, I won't feel guilty about how easy it is to keep a clean house, and I'll smack the martyr in me (or give her an umbrella drink and sit her down outside in an Adirondack chair) and tell her to relax. Everything is done.

God bless you for helping us martyrs.

Fluttering again in Colorado

> ## "When you let go of your perfectionism, procrastination goes away."
> ## — FlyLady

DAY
23

Add an Afternoon Routine.
Start dinner, help with homework,
and empty lunch box.

Afternoons are Made for Fun and Getting Stuff Done

Our routines don't come naturally to us, but we are smart and we can learn anything put in front of us, if we want to! You found FlyLady because you were looking for a way to get your home clean. You heard that we teach you how to clean; well that is not exactly the truth. Most of us have been taught how to clean by forced labor of trial and error when we were children. You know the drill; if you don't clean it right then you are going to have to redo it! There is another order yelled at us and we were just children: GO CLEAN YOUR ROOM. The sad part was that we didn't know where to start. We were told to do it, yet no one ever took the time to teach us how to do it.

Now let me take up for our parents. If they were messy like us, then they were not taught either and if they were Born Organized they didn't know how to teach us because it was second nature to them. So, you see we missed out on both counts. We have had to learn how to clean all by ourselves. Cleaning is the easy part. It is the routines that are the part that Born Organized folks couldn't teach us. If you watch a Born Organized person, they putter around all day. They always have something to do. They actually see things to do. We are immune to many of those things until the mess gets so bad, that we can't stand it another day and then we hear our Momma's voice coming out of our mouths, "GO CLEAN YOUR ROOM!"

What we teach you is to relieve the stress of life by establishing simple habits and to string them into a peaceful dance to help you glide through your day. Doesn't that just sound sweet? These little habits become automatic like our born organized family member's habits. The difference is we have made a conscious effort to build these habits. We CAN learn new tricks when the student is ready and it is your idea. The secret is making it fun for you.

All we have ever wanted to do is just go out and play. Our routines free us to FLY! Routines get things done so we can have more fun and enjoy our home and our families. Do you remember coming home from school and having to change clothes before you went outside to play? We also had to get our homework finished. This is why we need an afternoon routine.

There are three types of afternoon routines: One for those who work outside the home, another for those who work at home, and one for when the children finish with school. Make sure your afternoon routine reminds you to eat lunch and drink your water. After all, if you don't take care of you, who will? This is a checklist of things to remind us: finish the laundry, start dinner, clean out the backpacks and lunch boxes, add appointments to your calendar, and help with homework.

This routine guides us into our evenings with less stress! Write them down so you don't have to remember them. Put them on Post-It Notes, note cards, or pretty sheets of paper. Don't obsess about them being perfect. I keep mine in a little photo album but they started as Post-It Notes on my bathroom mirror! This way you have a simple guide for your day; a small morning routine, afternoon, and then an evening routine. Make our routines yours. Adapt them for your family and put them in a simple control journal, but don't make them so large that you crash and burn.

No Longer Sucked in by Reality Television

Dear FlyLady,

I just wanted to share with you that I was working on my afternoon routine today when I noticed there was a television show coming on about how to get your life in control, lose the clutter, be less stressed, and less anxious. This is the type of show that would normally stop me dead in my tracks and cause me to lounge on the couch for an hour riveted to the television. Not this time. For the first time in my ten years of marriage (when all my clutter and chaos really started bothering me), I felt like I already had found the answer to this problem and didn't need to listen. WOW!! What a revelation.

I have been flying since the beginning of January and am getting off to a good start. I have my routines down and my sink is shining most of the time (no longer piled high with dishes each night) and my laundry is getting more and more under control as time goes by.

In fact, my mom came to visit last week and I didn't even have to do a two day cleaning marathon like I normally do. About two hours before her plane was to arrive, I quickly dusted, vacuumed, swept and mopped the kitchen floor and I was ready for her. It was so freeing. What a blessing you are to me!

Thank you so much for sharing your expertise with those of us who are in such need of it. Your instruction has really turned my life around.

Learning to Fly in Texas

"Our routines free us to FLY!"

— FlyLady

Day 23

DAY
24

Add Swish and Swipe to your
Morning Routine. This keeps your
bathroom company ready!

Feel Like a Queen in Your Own Home

As part of my morning routine, I clean my bathroom every day. Now this is not crisis cleaning because company is coming and you have not touched the bathroom in months. This is a daily maintenance that keeps it company ready all the time! I know many of you don't think that this needs to be done but I assure you that you deserve a clean and fresh smelling bathroom all the time, too.

It doesn't take much time to do this, either. I call it a swish and a swipe. Doesn't that sound like a lick and a promise; quick and easy! Here is how it works and once you establish this habit, your bathroom will never look and smell dirty again. It takes me longer to explain how to swish and swipe than it does to do it.

To accomplish this, you need a couple of things to keep in your bathroom. I have my favorite window cleaner, Windex, in each bathroom just for this purpose along with one of our Purple Rags. You can use whatever you like, just so you don't have to leave the room to swish and swipe. No need to get sidetracked, if you will do this.

Here is the swipe part. I take the window cleaner and a purple rag to wipe off the mirror, the counter, faucets, and sink. Bam! it is just that fast! I do this while I am getting dressed and I put my things away. Do you hear me? Put your stuff away as you use it; this keeps your counter clear and easy to wipe down.

Then I take a wad of toilet paper and head toward the toilet. I keep a toilet bowl brush (Rubba Swisha) beside each toilet in our home. They are kept in a crock (one like you put kitchen utensils in) or a vase. In this crock, I keep a one to one solution of old shampoo or body wash (not bathroom caustic cleaner) and water in my holder. Soap is soap as far as I am concerned. You could use old bubble bath that you hate or whatever you have. Now don't do this if you have little children or pets that will get into this mixture.

Each morning, take the brush and let the excess cleaner drip off; if it is thick you may have to water down the solution a bit so it will drain well. Then take the Rubba Swisha and swish it around in the toilet. Then wipe off the back of the toilet with the rag, then the seat with toilet paper, the rim and lastly the sides and floor. If you have little boys, you know how they miss with their aim. When you do this once a day, you will find that your toilet is always fresh as a daisy.

There you have it, Swish and Swipe! This takes all of a minute from start to finish but you have to have everything in the bathroom so you have no excuses to not do this. Now go gather up an old vase for the bathroom and look in the bathroom closet for some shampoo or bubble bath that will work for swishing the toilet. Put your Purple Rag and Rubba Swisha in your bathroom so you can Swish and Swipe with ease! We have developed these wonderful tools to keep you motivated. They are available on our website.

The Swish and Swipe is the Greatest

Dear FlyLady,

I used to loathe cleaning the bathroom, particularly the shower and tub. I would let the bathroom get really bad and then do a marathon cleaning. I hated doing the marathon cleaning so I wouldn't do it again for a long time. These days, my bathroom is always clean. Just a quick swipe each day is all it takes; it's really true!

I wanted to share how I clean while I am in the shower and tub - the area I truly dreaded. I keep a Rubba Scrubba and a Purple Rag in the shower. The Rubba Scrubba cleans the caulk between the tub and shower walls. It's abrasive enough to clean it, but gentle enough not to tear it. I use the Purple Rag to wipe down the shower walls and tub. It works better than anything I have tried. The rag grabs the soap scum and lifts it right off. It also shines the faucets beautifully. Now, this may sound weird, but I put the rag on the floor of the tub and move it around with my foot while showering. Believe it or not, it cleans the bottom of the tub with the greatest of ease.

Thanks to you I always have a clean bathroom and I enjoy keeping it clean.

Flybaby Chris in MN

"Nothing says "I LOVE YOU"

like a clean toilet

when you are sick!"

— FlyLady

Day 24

DAY
25

It takes a month to establish habits.

Be kind to you!

Give yourself a Gold Star!

It's All About the Routines

It takes us a month to establish a habit. I set it up this way because I knew that I would miss a day here and there and I didn't want to throw the baby out with the bath water. That was how I had always done it with my perfectionism. If I missed a day, I gave up. Well I factored this part of our personalities into our FlyLady system. This is why we take a whole month to establish one habit.

Do you remember when we were in first grade that we got gold stars for all sorts of things? Well I think that we each deserve a gold star, purple star, red star for whatever we see fit. Let's get ourselves some stars and have fun. I'll bet you probably have some around the house. If not, this week pick up some assorted sheets of stars to use on your calendar or better yet, let go of your perfectionism and just draw a star on your calendar.

Pick out one habit you are trying to establish and give yourself a star for doing it. Now don't throw in the towel if you miss a day! Just jump back in and look at what you have accomplished; not the missing star! Do you hear me! Your perfectionism can paralyze you if you let it! I am very proud of you for taking these BabySteps, signing up for our emails, and making the decision to get rid of the CHAOS in your life. BabySteps will get you there!

Go Me! 29 Gold Stars

Dear FlyLady,

I did it!! I really did it. After being a FlyBaby for several years I finally kept my sink shiny for 29 out of 31 days. Go me! Tomorrow I will clean off my kitchen table, add a centerpiece and that will be my new shiny sink. My goal is to keep the sink and table clean, shiny and clutter free for the month of February. The gold stars really do help.

Thank you FlyLady for all you do to help me not to live in chaos.

FlyBaby B

> **"We are here to lift you up and celebrate every little accomplishment!"**
> *— FlyLady*

DAY
26

Don't allow perfectionism
to beat you up if you miss a day!
You're not behind!

Make It Easy on Yourself

We are too hard on ourselves. Why do you think we make huge lists? We just keep piling on so that we can at least look productive even if we get too overwhelmed by the list to actually do anything on it! Suppose you DID get something done. We were all taught that everything unfinished on our "to do" list gets put on tomorrow's list. I am feeling sick, thinking about a list that continues to be so large that we can never seem to make any headway with it.

This is the reason I started by shining my sink! I knew that if I tried to do more for that month that I would give up again and throw in the towel for the very last time. I was so tired of being disorganized that I felt like such a failure. I needed something to make me feel better. I decided that I could do one little thing. I never dreamed that it would be the saving grace for me and thousands of others. We CAN accomplish something even if it is just one thing. From that simple beginning with my sink, the other habits came so easily. All the while I would keep reminding myself that I only had to do this one thing. As a habit becomes automatic, it is much easier to add one more item to your routine. This is how we all should be building our routines. It took me around nine months to fully incorporate my habits into routines that help me to dance through my day. I like to think of it as giving birth to the new me!

Shining my sink is one of the last things I do before I head off to get ready for bed. It is part of my before bed routine. Is your before bed routine getting to be too big? Are you skipping it all together to just crash into the bed? This is what happens when we don't pace ourselves and continue to pile on. Our bodies and our minds haven't had a chance to incorporate these simple BabySteps into the flow of our lives.

It takes about a month of practice for one habit to stick with you. I went for months with the steps to my routines on post-it notes all over the house. That is when I had the idea to build the control journal. There is just something about being able to mark it off your list and go to the next item. It is even better to do the whole routine and then mark everything off the list saying, "I DID THAT ALREADY!"

So why are you trying to make it so hard on yourself by doing too much too fast and feeling like a failure? Life is just too short! Do you hear me? Make it easy on yourself by starting small and building upon those firm foundations. I did it, and so can you, if you will let go of your "all or nothing thinking" and the way you continually punish yourself. Oh and don't you let perfectionism rear its ugly head again!

WE DON'T PUNISH OURSELVES ANY LONGER! We are FLYing now and when you are loving yourself, you will do your best to be kind to you! Make it easy on yourself! Try BabySteps!

The Prison of Perfectionism

Dear FlyLady,

I'm sure you've heard this countless times. But it won't hurt to hear one more time. Thank you for your daily encouragement and inspiration to love ourselves and the homes we live in by blessing it to be free from clutter. Thank you for reminding us that BabySteps can take on the whole world, one step at a time, and that perfectionism is a disease and a prison. Thank you for being you. May God bless you more and more and keep you smiling always!

New FlyBaby Christine

"It doesn't matter if you miss one day; just get back on your horse and keep taking those BabySteps."

— FlyLady

Day 26

DAY
27

What's for dinner?
If you think about this at 10:00 am,
you will know the answer!

Menu Planning Isn't Rocket Science

The other day I got a message that said for the first twenty years of a woman's life, she spends wanting to know who she is going to marry and the next twenty years trying to figure out what's for supper!

We have all stood in front of the refrigerator hoping that the cold air would somehow give us some inspiration about what to cook. The hard part of cooking is knowing what you are going to fix. It is only difficult if you wait till your family is hollering WHAT'S FOR DINNER?

Menu planning is not hard. We just have to quit procrastinating about it and sit down and do it. I like to have an outline for the week to plan my menus around.

Sunday: Chicken

Monday: Beef

Tuesday: Casserole or Pasta

Wednesday: Pork

Thursday: Soup and Sandwich

Friday: Date Night! We eat out!

Saturday: Pizza

Some members add an ethnic flair to their meal planning. Here is a twist on the weekly menu planning that I will be trying out:

Monday: MEXICAN tacos, fajitas, nacho platter, taco salad, burritos

Tuesday: ITALIAN pizza (frozen), spaghetti, linguine and clams, ravioli, gnocchi, gyros, anti-pasta, Italian hoagie or meatball sandwich

Wednesday: AMERICAN hot dogs, burgers, pork chops, wings, soup and sandwich, chicken nuggets

Thursday: ONE-DISH COOKING Crock Pot /Skillet dish/Casserole, Chicken and sauce in crock, Stir fry, homemade Tuna Helper dish, fried rice with shrimp

Friday: FISH Dine out or take-out fish sandwich or grill/bake fish at home, shrimp salad, tuna salad sandwich, anything seafood

Saturday and Sunday: depends on weekend plans. Possible small cooking session to prep for the week's dinners

Here is another way, too:

Sunday: Italian

Monday: Seafood

Tuesday: Meat

Wednesday: Anything

Thursday: Mexican

Friday: American

Saturday: Chinese

Then you could do it this way to get the family involved!:

Sunday: Cooks day off the crockpot does the work

Monday: Daddy's favorite

Tuesday: Kids cook with supervision

Wednesday: Mommy's favorite

Thursday: Family Favorite

Friday: Special meal: Candles and good dishes Date night!

Saturday: Family cook! Make pizzas or tacos

You see, this isn't rocket science if you will just sit down for 10 minutes and start getting creative. You can play with making sure each meal has all the different colors on the plate: Green stuff (salad), White stuff (bread), Yellow/orange stuff (veggies), Red stuff (fruit or veggies). Have fun!

When you are making your menus and grocery lists, please don't forget the breakfast and lunches that you have to fix. Utilize a calendar to help you with your menu planning. This is a brilliant tip from a FlyBaby. Take a Post-It Note and cut off the sticky part so that you have a small strip. Then write your dinner entrée on the strip and place it on the day of the week that fits your family's schedule. At the end of the week, peel off each dinner and bump it up a few weeks on your calendar to a new date, unless no one liked it. Then when it is time to menu plan for a future week, several days are already planned! Also, you can switch around the dinners in one week if you need to because you don't have all you need for the recipe.

Knowing What's for Dinner Is Empowering!

Just this morning my hungry three-year-old boy woke me up asking, "What's for dinner?" How pleased I was to have an answer, down to the potatoes and salad on the side.

One side-benefit of having a meal plan is that I have been able to involve my busy seven-year-old in dinner preparation. She loves to cook, and I want to nurture this instinct. The time between arriving home from school and dinner time is a busy time for her to snack, to play, and to do homework.

Now that I have a dinner plan, I can take five to ten minutes AFTER dinner to prepare the next night's dinner with her. She has been eating much better at dinner time now that she is a part of dinner preparation. Even more, she has become an ally in getting my smaller children to try new food. I heard her saying, "There's mustard in the sauce, but you won't even mind it with all the orange juice." She knew that because she had added the mustard, stirred the sauce, and tasted it the night before.

I have also been keeping my sink clean during the day. Sometimes I have to force myself, saying, "Just put away five dishes!" But once I get going, I usually end with a shiny sink. Here is the extra perk; my husband, who usually cleans up the dinner dishes, has started running and EMPTYING the dishwasher at night. What a boost in the morning.

Many thanks for your encouragement and your great ideas.

Amy in New Jersey

> ## "You are really gonna FLY
> ## when you know
> ## what's for dinner!"
> ## — FlyLady

DAY
28

If you don't take care
of you, who will?
Eat healthy food
and drink your water!

If You Don't Take Care of You, Who Will?

Let me tell you about FLYing! Many years ago, I started to practice loving myself. At first in words only. I would meditate and instead of having a mantra (I didn't even know what that was and didn't care), I knew I needed some words to help me focus. I chose," I love myself!" As I would breathe in, I would say "I love" and as I would breathe out, I would say, "my-self". I would say it over and over. Eventually each time I would close my eyes, those words would pop into my head.

Soon I was doing things to love myself: getting my rest, taking bubble baths, reading books I enjoyed, spending time with friends who uplifted me, getting dressed every day, and putting on makeup. By this time, I was able to look into the mirror and not look away or find fault with my face. I was loving myself with actions.

Our message is about so much more than cleaning your home. If we do nothing else, I hope we impress upon you that if you don't take care of yourself, you will have nothing left to nurture your family. You cannot fill their cups with an empty pitcher. Everyone will be left unfulfilled. You have found us, because you were searching for something, anything to help you get your home in order.

The truth is, like Dorothy from the Wizard of Oz, you have had the power inside yourself all of this time. Your journey home is almost complete. Only a few more steps in your ruby slippers (routines and shoes) and you will find the peace you have been searching for your whole life. I know this sounds too simple to be true, but I promise that if you will take care of yourself first the house will come together like magic before your very eyes. If you don't believe me, then try to prove me wrong. Put down those excuses that have led you down the wrong path and focus on your goal. Use this system to guide you to your special place of peace. You will find it. Come FLY with me.

Not Perfect Enough

Dear FlyLady,

It seems like I have been a hostage most of my adult life. My mother was a wonderful homemaker and still prides herself on making wonderful food and welcoming people into her home. I've always been down on myself because I am not like her. I work full time and have three children, yet even though I know how to make wonderful food I don't; and welcoming people in my home is just too much work. My house keeping is far from perfect and I didn't feel it was perfect enough to invite people inside.

I've literally made myself physically ill because I've tried to do it all. And guess who wasn't taken care of in the least: me. I'm now visiting a doctor and starting to take care of myself; but it will be a long road to recovery because I have neglected taking care of me because I was trying to be perfect and do it all. I then came to the realization I can't, but surprise my children and my husband still love me!

I may still be a FlyBaby in many ways. I thank you for your wonderful message to so many women who we don't have to be perfect. The idea that we are supposed to do it all comes from within and from programming we've listened to all of our lives. I pray my daughter will grow up with knowing that she does not have to be perfect or do it all. I guess she now has her mother to be an example. Thank you again.

May Blessings Abound,

FlyBaby Beverly

"We give so much of ourselves away every day; it is not selfish to take a few minutes to fill your heart with joy!"
— *FlyLady*

DAY
29

With BabySteps,
you've learned the basics of FLYing.

Progress not Perfection!

We are Survivors

From the day we were born we have had perfectionism shoved down our throats. You know those words as well as I do, "If you can't do it right then don't do it at all!" We were also forced to redo things when we didn't do them to suit the person giving the ORDERS!

None of us like to be dictated to! What we were taught by these words and actions is that it didn't matter how well we did something because it was never going to live up to the expectations of that person we were trying to please. Do you want to know what happened then? We gave up! We didn't even try anymore because we knew it would not be good enough.

This pattern of being put down was all you heard. That is why we feel the need to beat ourselves up when we don't do something right! This negative attitude was drilled into our heads. We were brainwashed with this perfectionism. Now, in our parents' defense, they had the same thing done to them. It is all they knew! We can put a stop to this vicious cycle of perfectionism through the generations.

We are our own person and we have made a choice to change. We are not being dictated to by our parents any longer. You may have just gotten fed up with living in CHAOS (Can't Have Anyone Over Syndrome) or you may have heard about this FlyLady person who can help you get your house clean. Whatever the reason, you are ready to try something new. This time the choice is yours!

When we get to make the decision, it is much easier for us to do! The only problem is that we still have those negative voices echoing in our heads. This is why we beat ourselves up! It is those voices from the past that make FLYing difficult! They tell us the same old message we have heard from day one! You have to do it perfectly or don't do it. So when you are not FLYing the way you think you are supposed to then you quit trying. This is also why we get overwhelmed!

In the perfectionism, we had forced on us, we look at the whole picture instead of just doing something. We don't think that 15 minutes can make a difference in a messy house. This goes back to getting it done right. We expect ourselves to magically do it all in one day! We are not Superwomen! This negativity ping-ponging in our heads tells us that we don't have time!

The real thing we are saying is not that we don't have time, but that we don't have time to do it right! This is when we begin to do what has always been done to us! We beat ourselves up or we punish ourselves. Because of this perfectionism, we don't feel worthy!

We don't feel worthy to have nice things. We don't feel worthy to live in peace. We don't feel worthy to enjoy ourselves and worst of all, we don't feel worthy to be loved! I want to help you eliminate those thoughts from your mind. I want to replace them with loving thoughts and rewards for taking BabySteps.

Your home did not get messy in a day and it is not going to get clean overnight. We are not our mothers and fathers. I don't expect you to be perfect! Quit expecting perfection from your precious little inner child. When you start feeling defeated, overwhelmed and beaten down, I want you to recognize the voices you are hearing in your head. Then say delete, delete, delete!

You can do this! I am so proud of you for taking the time to read this God Breeze Hurricane! You are worthy of being loved! I will start this ball rolling by saying there is no wrong way or right way to FLY; there is only your way! It all starts by going to shine your sink and Finally Loving Yourself by not beating yourself up when you are not perfect! Nobody is ever perfect!

Every BabyStep Helped My Confidence

Dear FlyLady,

In the last 6 months, your BabySteps and encouragement have taken me from being a woman frozen by perfection to a woman who loves to bless her home! In the past, I tried several programs to help me clean my home. One that stands out in my memory had me go from room to room and make a list of everything that needed to be cleaned, and then make a master calendar of what needed to be done every day for a year.

Well, I love making lists and filling out calendars, so that was a breeze. However, on the first day I was to actually start cleaning; I looked at the list of things on the calendar and was paralyzed by it! How could I get all that stuff done and do it right in just one day? Needless to say, I put that calendar in the trash and felt like a failure.

Now, let me tell you my experience with FlyLady. On day one, I was instructed to empty my kitchen sink and shine it; then send an email to FlyLady that I'd done it. That was it! That was awesome! FlyLady told me how good it would make me feel, she told me she was proud of me; I felt successful!

Every BabyStep helped me grow more confident, getting dressed to shoes (no problem), swish and swipe the bathroom (easy), do a load of laundry (come on FlyLady, how about a challenge?), read your emails for inspiration (my pleasure), set my timer for 15 minutes (very motivating). I could go on and on.

Now I bless my home every day; no more cleaning, no more worrying about doing it the "right way." I just jump in where I am and love my home, my family, and myself! I really appreciate your dedication to us, men and women of all ages, who need help realizing that cleaning done incorrectly still blesses our families!

With love and prayers of gratitude,

FlyBaby Karen

"Now don't try to do a full-blown routine the very first night. Start small and build upon your new habits."
— *FlyLady*

DAY
30

To stay organized,
check your calendar twice a day.

Any upcoming Birthdays?

Developing Your Calendar Habits

Did you know that most FlyBabies are calendar challenged? It took me years and thousands of dollars to finally develop a system that worked for me. With every new system, I tried to get my home organized, I would buy a planner in hopes that it would somehow miraculously fix me. Guess what, it doesn't happen!

Many calendars are developed by naturally born organized people. These folks automatically know how to use one. If they came with directions, we wouldn't use the instructions anyway. Our system is a bit different. We teach you routines that actually tell you to open up your calendar and check your appointments. This seems strange for born organized people. They have never needed to be reminded to check their calendar. In fact, they think something is wrong with us, because we need this kind of prompting. Let me tell you one little thing: we are every bit as smart as the next person; we just have a little different way learning.

Habits come naturally to born organized people. We must practice and develop these habits. It took me thirty years to learn how to use a calendar. As I started adding one habit at a time to my daily routines, the calendar became an integral part of my planning for the next day.

In order to know what clothes to lay out for the next day, I had to know what was on my schedule for tomorrow. I would look at my calendar to check my appointments. Then the next morning I would recheck it, after all, I had slept and there is no telling what I had forgotten during the night. I would write it down in order not to have to remember and keep juggling bits of information in my brain. This relieves stress, especially if you only write these things in one place.

This is why we recommend using one family wall calendar, not three of them or twenty different slips of paper stashed in your purse, posted on the refrigerator or piled on a so-called desk that is a raging hot spot! We don't even care what kind of calendar you use, just that you practice using one. I have wasted a lot of money on planners/calendars, so I told myself that I would not buy anything else until I could develop the habits that would insure the calendar would be used instead of gathering dust. I started with a free calendar, you know the ones that you get as an advertisement at the beginning of a new year. I used this until my schedule became too big and I didn't have enough room to write my appointments.

We want to teach you how to use your calendar, but keep in mind it is a tool and a tool will do you no good if you don't learn how to use it properly. Checking your calendar is part of your morning and before bed routine.

As part of your basic weekly plan, we check our schedules with our family members to determine our menus for the next week and prepare our grocery list. You can also use it for bill paying and sending birthday cards. Your calendar will become your life-line if you will use it in conjunction with your control journal to act as your memory so you don't have to try and juggle all the information in your head.

These skills don't happen overnight. They take time to develop and implement. You can do this. Let me tell you, if I can do this after 30 years of being calendar challenged, you can, too.

I want for you what I have and it is a peace that comes from not missing an appointment, paying my bills on time, and knowing that I haven't forgotten some important date. You can have this, too. Follow our directions and you will find yourself FLYing before you know it. BabySteps will get you there. I promise. Are you ready to FLY with your Calendar guiding you every step of the way?

Teaching My Daughter to Use a Calendar

Dear FlyLady,

I feel so awesome right now that I just have to share this with you. I have been a FlyBaby for about 3-4 years. I am still learning and practicing, but I have come a long, long way. I am also trying to teach my 4-year-old daughter to FLY by using the calendar and routines to keep organized.

When she started preschool this year, we immediately put all of her holidays on the calendar. As school goes on, we add any due dates that we learn of to the calendar right away. Love that FlyLady calendar - lots of room for everything! Anyway, we also wrote out a routine for getting ready for preschool (brush hair, brush teeth, do we need to return anything, do we need snow pants, etc.). We printed it and put it in a page protector. Every single day we check the calendar and run through the checklist.

Today, when we arrived at preschool, one mom said they forgot their library book (Thursday is library day) and another mother told her son he would have to wear his boots today because they forgot his tennis shoes. My daughter had her tennis shoes to change into and she had her library book - all because of the calendar and checklist. I thought to myself, "Thank you FlyLady!"

With much gratitude,

FlyBaby Chris in MN

> **"Make a family rule; if you don't put it on the calendar, it won't happen. Developing effective calendar habits is going to reduce your stress!"**
> **— *FlyLady***

Day 30

DAY

31

I'm so proud of you!

Keep decluttering!

Get signed up for our messages.

You're FLYing now!

Good Enough is Good Enough

Our precious little princess inside of us just really wants to be loved! She has tried so hard for acceptance and most of her life she has been told, in many different ways, that she was not good enough. Eventually the little child just gives up!

Did this happen to you? Were you forced to wash dishes over and over? Were you told to clean your room only to have your mother or father come in and do it for you by throwing your stuff away? Can you see how we rebelled against this lack of acceptance? We quit trying. We knew it would never be good enough, so why bother.

I just want to hold that precious little child and tell her that she is loved and show her that she is good enough and is worthy to have a home that blesses her. We have had housework used as punishment. No wonder we didn't want to do it. I have gotten emails where a FlyBaby found herself standing at the sink sobbing. She wasn't even upset. She was just crying. Now I am not a psychologist or a doctor but do you think she could have been having a flashback with a traumatic incident from her past. She said, when she was a child, she was punished with washing the dishes.

What did we have done to us? What have we done to our children because of that? We have the ability to re-parent ourselves. The hardest part in letting go of our perfectionism is saying "Good Enough" is "Good Enough"! This goes against everything we were taught, everything we were tortured with, and everything we have crammed down our throats from the first day we were born!

Our poor little child within us tried so hard to live up to those unrealistic standards. Even when we did our best, it was never "Good Enough"! We may not have been told that in words but their actions would speak much louder than the words that were never said.

Perfectionism is a parasite that feeds off the love we didn't receive. It establishes residence in its host the first day that little child gets crushed. From that day forward, perfectionism has its hold on us. Then we pass it on to our children. Mv goal is to rid our bodies of this vicious cunning chameleon-like parasite and keep it from taking root in our children and grandchildren.

Perfection is something that we are taught is supposed to be a good thing! When you look hard at it, you can see that it is a disguise that either makes you give up before you start or it pushes you to exhaustion. That little child only wants to be loved so she just works and works for that praise, only to have her little bubble burst. Then she says why bother because it will never be good enough.

Are you ready to expel the perfectionism parasite and not infect others with it? It starts with forgiveness. Our parents had this done to them, too. We can stop it right here and right now!

Release your CHAOS, one BabyStep at a time!

FlyLady Is Like A Mother To Me!

I have been using your system now for a couple of months, after having gone several years of trying FlyLady and crashing, because I wanted everything to get done NOW! I think that is the hardest thing, is to want to get it all done at once. I was never taught growing up to establish routines, and to do things a little at a time. It was always, work like mad until I dropped (literally!). If I didn't have time to do something and to do it perfectly, it didn't get done.

Well, I am learning to just take things little by little, and it is so much more peaceful and less stressful! It is hard sometimes, because my old perfectionism wants to come back and beat me up! Sometimes we are our own worst enemies! I have eight children, and I really want to teach them not to crash and burn, like I so often do, and they have, too. I want to teach them to establish routines, so that their rooms won't be a disaster site, and so that one day their homes won't be a disaster site! Nagging my children to get things done, and get it done NOW is like pushing a car uphill that is put into reverse!

I am telling you right now, that you are like a mother to me! Your e-mails tell me what to do to keep me on track, and encourage me to keep on. You pick me up when I am discouraged and feel like throwing in the towel! Thanks for the common-sense advice about wearing lace-up shoes, doing 5-minute room rescues, 15-min hot spots, and just doing our best and not beating ourselves up if it is not perfect! I just want to give you a BIG hug right now! Thanks for all your "mothering" that you do for all of us struggling FlyBabies!

Love,

An Iowa FlyBaby

"Even though I can't be there to give you a hug, I want you to know that I am very proud of you."
— FlyLady

Day 31

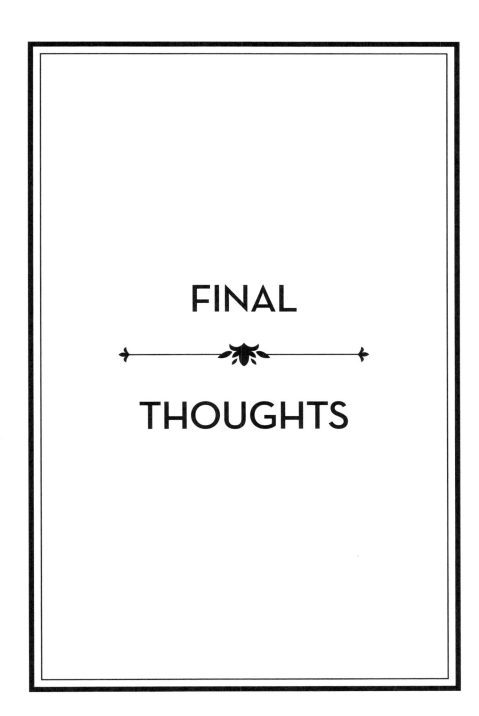

FINAL

THOUGHTS

CHAOS to Clean

For those of you who read this little book one day at a time, you have experienced just a small taste of what FLYing is all about. The rest of you who kept reading till the end and are now ready to put the book down and never even attempt any of the BabySteps, this is your perfectionism! You had to see how it all fits together before you could ever get started. You are not alone.

The whole FlyLady System is based upon taking BabySteps. You have just read our immersion version. This is to day-by-day introduce you to another feature. With our perfectionism, we can't wait to get started, so we read the whole book. At that point, your head is spinning and you are too overwhelmed to even start. BabySteps work, when you are kind to yourself.

I have suffered with this my whole life. It was only when I recognized how mean I was to myself over simple things that I found a way to get organized. In my perfectionism, I was expecting myself to absorb everything and be organized right out of the gate. That is not how our minds and bodies work.

We need to establish simple habits one at a time then string them into routines. With our perfectionism, we want what we want, and we expect it to happen right now. In the real world, it takes time to develop new habits. Psychologists tell us that it takes twenty-one days. You know what happens if you miss a day! Your perfectionism kicks in and you beat yourself up. Then you toss a simple system out the door because you have messed up. Now that you have been through our immersion class, this is just the beginning. Keep in mind you are not behind; jump in where you are.

In this overview, we have explained our system but now it is time to develop these simple habits and string them into routines. Through this process, you have built the beginnings of your Control Journal. It is just a place to hold your habits and routines. It is sort of like having an instruction manual for your home. If the truth be told, it is so we don't have to remember everything at one time. It is our guide to how our home runs on automatic pilot. This is the beauty of having a control journal; anyone can step in and help you if there is an emergency.

Please be kind to yourself! I want for you what I have found with this system! Peace! It took me nine months of decluttering every day and establishing my habits to give birth to a new way of living! Let go of your perfectionism and find this peace for yourself. You can do this! Progress not Perfection!